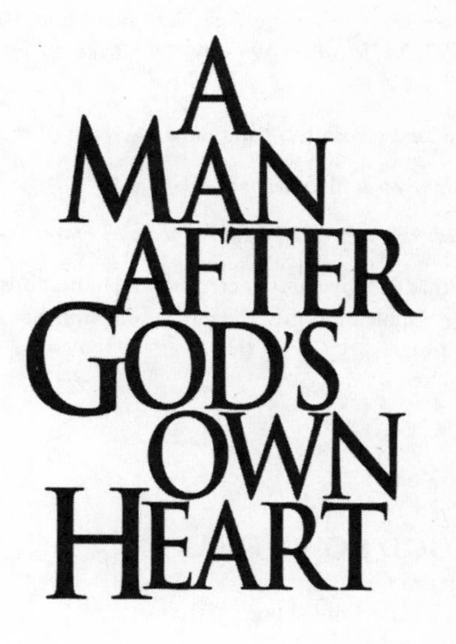

JIM GEORGE

HARVEST HOUSE PUBLISHERS
EUGENE, OREGON

Cover by Garborg Design Works, Minneapolis, Minnesota

Cover photo © Allioy Photography / Veer; Author photo by Harry Langdon

Every effort has been made to give proper credit for all quotations. If for any reason proper credit has not been given, please notify the author or publisher and proper notation will be given on future printing.

A MAN AFTER GOD'S OWN HEART

Published by Harvest House Publishers
Eugene, OR 97402
www.harvesthousepublishers.com

ISBN 978-0-7369-2296-8 (pbk.)
ISBN 978-0-7369-3213-4 (eBook)

Library of Congress Cataloging-in-Publication Data
George, Jim, 1943–
A man after God's own heart / Jim George.
p. cm.
Includes bibliographical references.
1. Christian men—Religious life. I. Title.
BV4528.2 .G46 2002
248.8'42—dc21 2002003156

Printed in the United States of America

12 13 14 15 16 17 18 19 / LB-MS / 14 13 12 11 10 9 8 7

For my two Pauls—
Paul Seitz
and
Paul Zaengle,
the best two sons-in-law
a man could ever have.
May you continue to be
godly husbands, fathers, and spiritual leaders,
and men after God's own heart.

Acknowledgment

My heartfelt thanks to Steve Miller,
friend, encourager, and
a true man after God's own heart.

Contents

A Word of Welcome

Every major accomplishment in a man's life requires a major level of commitment. I'm sure you can remember such an accomplishment in your life. Perhaps you were starting your own business. Or maybe you were contemplating a job change or mapping out a new direction for your company or your family. Whatever it was, there was probably some initial hesitancy. One day you were eager to start...and the next day you weren't so sure. But once you made the decision to proceed, all the long hours of effort were worth it because of the joy of seeing the fruit of your labors.

Another man, King David, whose life is sprinkled throughout this book, understood this principle of commitment when he desired to buy land and build an altar to God. However, because David was the king, the landowner wanted to give him the land. But David realized that the greater the commitment, the greater would be the blessing. Therefore he declared, "I will not sacrifice to the Lord my God burnt offerings that cost me nothing" (2 Samuel 24:24).

I'm thrilled to have the opportunity to put the barebones principles of my 25-plus years of ministry to men in print. It's been a great privilege over the decades to teach, train, equip, disciple, counsel, and mentor many men using these principles from God's Word. And in the lives of man after man, these truths have reaped major blessings in his spiritual life, in his marriage and family, in his church, and on the job. Once any hurdles of hesitancy were dispelled and a decision was made to proceed full-speed ahead, all the effort was definitely worth it.

I invite you to embark with me on a journey toward greater growth and maturity. Join me in making giant strides toward becoming a man after God's own heart. Prepare yourself to learn about

- the priorities of a man after God's own heart,
- the practices of a man after God's own heart, and
- the person of King David, the original man after God's own heart.

You will reap major blessings in every area of your life as you make your own commitment to follow after God and to do everything He wants you to do (Acts 13:22).

May God encourage and strengthen you as you make the journey of your life—the journey to becoming a man after God's own heart.

Your fellow traveler,
Jim George

Part One

The Pursuit of God

In the Scriptures, God is frequently represented as searching for a man of a certain type. Not men, but a man. Not a group, but an individual.

When God does discover a man who conforms to His spiritual requirement, who is willing to pay the full price of discipleship, He uses him to the limit, despite his patent shortcomings.[1]

—J. OSWALD SANDERS

1
What Is Your Heart's Desire?

I have found David son of Jesse
a man after my own heart;
he will do everything I want him to do.

—Acts 13:22

When I was a young boy, my parents took me on our one and only family vacation. Leaving from my boyhood home of Miami, Oklahoma, we passed through Dodge City, Kansas, on our way to Colorado. And of course, we had to stop in this historic town and visit its famous Boot Hill Cemetery.

To this day I can still remember looking down at a tombstone with an inscription to this effect:

Here lies Old Joe.
He died with his boots on.

And at the end of the grave were two boots sticking up out of the earth! Later I learned that "Old Joe" wasn't actually buried there. And much later I found out that the inscription on a grave marker is called an *epitaph*, which is basically a short composition in prose or verse written as a tribute to a dead person.

Since that memorable visit to Boot Hill, I've collected a few other tributes. For instance, a Greek poet wrote this on the tomb of the Spartan heroes at Thermopylae in the fifth century B.C.:

Go, tell the Spartans, gentle passer-by,
That here, obedient to their law, we lie.

This next one was written in memory of the English poet Shakespeare:

He was not of an age, but for all time.

Having a bit of a background in science, I like what was written of a scientist who died at the age of 85:

He Died Learning

Most epitaphs are written by those who knew the deceased person. Benjamin Franklin, however, the famous American statesman, wrote his own tribute:

The body of B. Franklin,
Printer
Like the cover of an old book
Its contents torn out
And stript of its lettering and gilding
Lies here, food for worms.
But the work shall not be lost
For it will, as he believ'd, appear once more
In a new and more perfect edition
Corrected and amended
By the Author.[2]

Then there are some humorous epitaphs too, such as...

All dressed up and no place to go.

Or...

Remember, friend, when passing by,
As you are now, so once was I.
As I am now, soon you will be,
Prepare for death and follow me.

To which someone later added...

To follow you I'm not content.
Until I know which way you went.

The epitaph that, to me, is the most inspiring of all (and also the most perplexing) is found written in the Bible. It's a tribute to King David, one of the most famous individuals in the Old Testament. Of him God writes,

> I have found David son of Jesse a man after my own heart; he will do everything I want him to do (Acts 13:22).

What Can We Learn from David?

The life of David makes for a fascinating character study. His is one of those great "rags to riches" stories. David started out a shepherd boy and ended up as a king. He became a great warrior and consolidated the tiny nation of Israel into a powerful kingdom that ruled a large part of the Middle East during the tenth century B.C.

But with all his accomplishments, David's greatest claim to fame, so to speak, is God's epitaph, "I have found David...a man after my own heart."

As I said earlier, I find this statement perplexing! God is declaring His approval of David's heart and life. That is puzzling in light of the fact that David's actions weren't always godly. In case you're unfamiliar with David's life, let me give you a brief overview of his checkered history.

- David was a warrior who shed much blood (1 Chronicles 22:8).
- David committed adultery with a woman named Bathsheba (2 Samuel 11:4).
- David later found out that he had gotten Bathsheba pregnant. To solve his problem, David ordered Bathsheba's husband put into a forward battle position, where he was killed (2 Samuel 11:5-17).
- David had multiple wives (2 Samuel 3:1-5).
- David was a negligent father, and his family was plagued with strife and tragedy (2 Samuel 13:15-18, 28-29; 18:33).
- Contrary to the Lord's command, David pridefully numbered his troops, causing 70,000 of his people to die in a plague (2 Samuel 24:10,15).

And yet God states, "I have found David...a man after my own heart." How can that be? How could God possibly commend a man with this kind of background?

Yes, David was a man with feet of clay, a man who at times committed sins that most of us could not imagine, let alone commit. Yet, over the long haul, David sought to be righteous and his heart's desire was to do God's will. This is the kind of man God looks for, as indicated by Jeremiah 5:1-9. God doesn't expect perfection, as we can clearly see from David. With all that David had done wrong in his life, God could still look at David's heart and say he was a man after His own heart—a man who did all God's will.

The Enabling Grace of God

This, my friend, is the grace of God. There can be no other explanation! By his actions, David didn't deserve God's blessings. But in his heart he had the right desire—a longing to follow and please God.

That brings me to an important question—one that can lead to a lot of meaning, purpose, and fulfillment in your life: Do *you* want to be a man after God's own heart? Or, put another way, is *your* heart's desire to follow after God?

You may think that's unrealistic because you have a tendency to take three steps forward then two steps back in your spiritual walk with God. You may imagine that being a man after God's own heart is too lofty a goal. You may conclude that it's not possible because of some of your past actions.

But you and I must never forget one thing: God looked at David's *heart*. And that's where God is going to look in our lives, too. When it comes to becoming a man after God's own heart, we can count on the grace of God—a grace that enables us and strengthens us at all times.

The Grace of God to John Newton

We can find encouragement in the grace God exhibited to another notable man. His name was John Newton (1725-1807). Your life couldn't be any worse than that of John Newton's. He was a rough, debauched slave trader who later described himself as a "wretch" who was lost and spiritually blind. But one day the grace of God used a fierce storm to put fear into the heart of this wicked slave merchant. According to Newton's testimony, that storm—along with his reading of the book *The Imitation of Christ* by Thomas à Kempis—led him to genuine conversion and brought a dramatic change in his heart and in his way of life.

John Newton never ceased to marvel at God's grace which had transformed him so completely. To express that marvelous grace, Newton wrote the now-famous hymn "Amazing Grace":

> Amazing grace, how sweet the sound
> That saved a wretch like me!
> I once was lost, but now am found,
> Was blind, but now I see.
> 'Twas grace that taught my heart to fear,
> And grace my fears relieved;
> How precious did that grace appear
> The hour I first believed![3]

Shortly before his death at age 82, John Newton is quoted as proclaiming with a loud voice during a message he was giving, "My memory is nearly gone, but I remember two things: That I am a great sinner, and that Christ is a great Savior!"

Now *that's* the cry of a man after God's own heart! You see, God looked at John Newton's heart, just as He looked at David's. And, my friend, that's where He's going to look in your life, too.

The Grace of God to You

Let's get very serious here for a moment. I want us to ask some hard questions:

Question #1—When God looks at your life, what does He look for? He doesn't look for perfection. Being a Christian is not about being perfect. The Bible says that there are no perfect men—no, not one (Romans 3:10). Like David, and like John

Newton, every person has sinned. Every person has disobeyed God. And it's this disobedience that separates us from God.

That's the bad news, but now for the good news! The only perfect man who ever walked the face of the earth was Jesus Christ, God's only Son. He was truly a man after God's own heart. In every way and at all times, He did everything exactly as the Father wanted Him to. At Jesus' baptism, God the Father testified of this when He said, "This is my Son, whom I love; with him I am well pleased" (Matthew 3:17).

Because Jesus was perfect and knew no sin, He was able to die for your sins and mine and pay the penalty for sin, which is death. The Bible tells us that "while we were still sinners, Christ died for us" (Romans 5:8). He was the perfect sacrifice for our sins. Because of what He did, we can be cleansed of sin and "approach the throne of *grace* with confidence, so that we may receive mercy and may find *grace* to help us in our time of need" (Hebrews 4:16, emphases added).

Question #2—What does it mean to become a Christian? Briefly, becoming a Christian means…

looking to God and His grace (Ephesians 2:8-9),

repenting of or turning away from our sins,

accepting God's gift of eternal life through His Son's death on our behalf,

receiving God's mercy and forgiveness, and…

living by His grace.

Being a Christian doesn't mean you and I don't sin anymore. We will still sin, but sin will cease to be the predominant pattern of our lives. That's because as Christians, we are new creatures in Christ (2 Corinthians 5:17). We are new children of God. And when we do sin, because the Holy

Spirit lives in us, we are convicted and possess a desire to repent so that the joy of our fellowship with God can be restored (Psalm 51:12).

Question #3—What is your heart's desire? We have looked at David's heart and his desire to follow God. We have looked at how John Newton came to recognize God's grace and how his heart changed. What about your own heart? Can God look at your heart and say, "I have found you to be a man after My heart who desires to do all My will"?

Question #4—Have you received Jesus as the Savior and Lord of your life? Perhaps you have already taken that step of faith and received Christ as your Savior. If not, this is truly the first step toward becoming a man after God's own heart. If you have not yet become a Christian, you can take this most important step in life with a prayer like this one:

> Jesus, I know I am a sinner, and I want to repent of my sins and turn and follow You. I believe that You died for my sins and rose again victorious over the power of sin and death, and I want to accept You as my personal Savior. Come into my life, Lord Jesus, and help me follow and obey You from this day forward. Amen.

Now, my friend, if you are a Christian, this epitaph found in a graveyard in England could be written of you:

I have sinned;
I have repented;
I have trusted;
I have loved;
I rest;
I shall rise;
I shall reign.[4]

Just as water is the only thing that can relieve thirst in the desert, the provision of God's Word is the only thing that can satisfy our spiritual thirst. It's the only thing that can give us encouragement in times of trial and direction for our busy lives.

—Jim George

2
Desiring Spiritual Growth

As the deer pants for streams of water,
so my soul pants for you, O God.
My soul thirsts for God, for the living God.

—Psalm 42:1-2

One summer some years ago I was privileged to be part of a team that conducted leadership conferences for pastors in the major cities of Australia. I'll never forget our first conference in Brisbane, Northern Australia. Brisbane is a beautiful city that basks in a pleasant semitropical climate with palm trees lining the streets and pineapples growing in fields along the roads leading to the countryside.

While staying in Brisbane, I was introduced to the Great Barrier Reef, which is famous among divers and snorkelers because of its crystal-clear blue waters. This famous reef extends for some 1,260 miles along the northeast coast above Brisbane. Its width varies from 10 to 90 miles wide. This massive and imposing barrier was produced, strangely enough, by tiny sea creatures called *coral.* These little animals live and die in colonies which, over the centuries, have built this amazing coral reef, parts of which are hundreds of feet deep.

Now, the Great Barrier Reef doesn't look alive. But because experts tell me that this astonishing reef is alive and is even continuing to grow as these tiny organisms live and die, I accept it as fact and marvel at what has been and is being produced.

Our Source of Growth

In a similar way, the Bible is amazing, too! At first glance, it looks like any other book. The pages have black ink on white paper, like the newspaper or the TV guide. And yet there is something very different and very alive about the Bible. Why is the Bible unique?

Claim #1—The Bible claims to be the Word of God, which makes it the best possible source for learning the ways of God: "All Scripture is God-breathed and is useful for teaching, rebuking, correcting and training in righteousness" (2 Timothy 3:16).

Claim #2—The Bible claims to be true and never tries to justify its statements. You would assume that if the Bible is God's Word to us (Claim #1), we could also be assured of its truthfulness to us. Indeed, the psalmist wrote, "The law of the LORD is perfect" (Psalm 19:7). So, we can trust the Bible to give us correct advice for life and living.

Claim #3—The Bible claims to be alive. Consider this amazing statement: "For the word of God is living and active. Sharper than any double-edged sword, it penetrates even to dividing soul and spirit, joints and marrow; it judges the thoughts and attitudes of the heart" (Hebrews 4:12).

With claims like these, you and I should take special note and be at least a little curious as to what the Bible has to say about life and our priorities. I know that when I read the Bible, my life is transformed. I think differently. I act differently. I talk differently. No other book has the same effect on a person as the Bible! We can read books on any subject and receive information that will help us in one way or another. But when it comes to the heart and soul, only the Bible can bring true and lasting changes.

More importantly, if the Bible is God's own Word, and if you and I want to live as men after God's own heart, then there's no better place for us to go for guidance. Don't you agree? God wrote the Bible to tell us about His love for us and to show us how we can enjoy an active, meaningful relationship with Him. He also lets us know how we can best live our lives and the priorities that lead to fulfilled living. So if your desire is to be a man after God's heart, you'll want to learn what these priorities are. That, of course, will mean taking the time to read the Bible.

The Encouragement to Grow

We naturally tend to consider it a tragedy when someone doesn't grow physically. But equally tragic is a Christian who is not growing spiritually or whose spiritual growth has been stunted. You see, brother, God desires for us to grow. In the Bible, growth is seen as a naturally occurring by-product of our life in Christ. In fact, we are commanded to "grow in the grace and knowledge of our Lord and Savior Jesus Christ" (2 Peter 3:18). The writer of the book of Hebrews also assumed that with the passing of time his readers would grow to the point where they could be teaching others the basics of God's Word. But he had to rebuke his readers because they hadn't grown (Hebrews 5:12). As I said, spiritual growth should be a *naturally* occurring by-product of our life in Christ.

Thirsting for Growth

Several years before retirement, I volunteered for a two-week assignment with my Army Reserve Unit in support of a massive war game in California's Mojave Desert. After 20 years of Army service, I knew that this field exercise would be demanding. I also knew I shouldn't have volunteered, but I did! So there I was, commanding a medical team supporting one of the tank units...and it was August...with 120-degree weather. The heat was oppressive. All I could think about was water, water, and more water! My body craved that life-giving substance.

Friend, the desire I had for water during those days is the kind of thirst we ought to have for God's Word. Our physical body knows that it cannot function without physical water. So, too, our spiritual being should realize that it can't function without the "living water" of God's Word. The psalmist described this craving for God in this way:

> As the deer pants for streams of water, so my soul pants for you, O God. My soul thirsts for God, for the living God (Psalm 42:1-2).

Do you have this kind of craving for God and His Word? Just as water is the only thing that can relieve our thirst in the desert, God's Word is the only thing that can satisfy our spiritual thirst. Only God's Word can give us encouragement in times of trial and clear direction when we're sifting through the chaos of our busy lives.

By the way, when it comes to spiritual growth, God doesn't leave you completely on your own. God's Spirit, who lives inside every believer, gives you the power and the desire to grow. Jesus promised that the Spirit will be your Guide and your Helper (John 14:16-17, 26).

Between the Bible and the Holy Spirit, God has given you all you need for spiritual growth. Is the craving there? Why not satisfy it by spending more time with God in His Word? My prayer is that as you read this book, your hunger and thirst for God and your desire for His Word will grow.

A Personal Story About Growth

Earlier I mentioned that it's unfortunate when someone's physical growth is hindered by disease or by an accident. And stunted spiritual growth is tragic, too. Well, I am among those who, when I was young, went to church regularly…but that was it. So when this spiritually immature country boy went away to college, I was a prime candidate for a spiritual fall. I was similar to the "lost son" in the story Jesus told in Luke 15, who…

> …got together all he had, set off for a distant country and there squandered his wealth in wild living…. When he came to his senses, he said, "…I will set out and go back to my father and say to him: Father, I have sinned against heaven and against you. I am no longer worthy to be called your son" (verses 11-19).

Like this young son, I came to my senses at about age 30 and realized I was starving to death spiritually. I, too, looked up and came back to my heavenly Father. And, like the father in the story who was "filled with compassion," God received me back (as He does anyone who comes to his or her senses and turns back to Him).

Realizing that I had wasted more than a decade of living in "a distant country," I was eager to learn God's Word and grow spiritually. I started reading through my Bible, beginning in Genesis 1, verse 1. Up to that time, I had never read through my Bible even once!

Like a man whose arm or leg has withered because of disability, my soul had withered because of the debilitating effects of sin. And like a man who starts up a physical therapy regimen designed to help him regain the use of an arm or a leg, I started "spiritual therapy" to regain my former strength, build even greater spiritual muscle, and, by God's grace, become useful to my heavenly Father. That was the desire of my grateful and penitent heart!

What about you? Is your story similar to mine? Have you lived or are you living in "a distant country" spiritually? If so, my hope is that you can recognize the value of desiring spiritual therapy or adhering to a spiritual regimen that will help you grow spiritually and strengthen your spiritual muscles. God desires that for you as His child. Do *you* desire that as well?

The Impact of Growth

What's remarkable about spiritual growth is the way it can impact every area of our lives. Not only will you and I be pleasing God and maturing as Christians, but we'll also see a significant positive effect on our relationships with others. Each of us, as a Christian man, husband, father, and worker, has contact with many people—people whose lives we can impact if we grow.

Now for a few questions about your growth:

Do you want to be a strong, maturing man of God? Then take care of your first priority, which is to develop a closer relationship with God.

Do you want to be a good husband? Through your time spent with God and His Word, you will find the answers to everything you need to know about loving and caring for your wife.

Do you want to be a good father? Then cultivate a friendship with God that seeks to depend upon His Word for wisdom. This intimacy with your Father in heaven will give you the wisdom you need for raising your children.

Do you care about your coworkers? If so, you'll want to have the kind of relationship with God that allows the Spirit of God to work through your life and point others to Him.

Do you want your life to count? I know I do. And I believe you do, too! If you are ready to begin the growth process that will ensure that your life does count, then the place to start is with God. You need to tell Him of your renewed or reinvigorated desire to grow spiritually.

An Example of Growth

You've probably heard of John Wesley. This man after God's own heart lived in the 1700s, and, along with his brother Charles, founded the Methodist Church. His life was one of great achievement as a result of dedicating himself to teaching God's Word to others. Because of his devotion to the Bible, John Wesley became known as a "man of one book"—*the* Book. He laid hold of the Bible because his heart's desire was to grow...and the Bible laid hold of him as well.

Every year, John Wesley and his followers would extend to God this prayer written by Wesley as a covenant to God expressing their desire to grow. If you would like to do so, you can make this your prayer for growth, too.

> O blessed Jesus...because You have been pleased to give me your holy laws as the Rule of my life...I do here willingly put my neck under your yoke, and set my shoulder to your burden...And subscribing to all your laws as holy, just, and good, I solemnly take them as the Rule of my words, thoughts, and actions; promising that...I will endeavor to order and govern my whole life according to your direction, and will not allow myself in the neglect of any thing that I know to be my duty.[5]

By committing yourself to growing spiritually and, by God's grace, living as a man after God's own heart, you'll become a man of God who is eager to fulfill all the roles and responsibilities that God has placed before you.

piritual growth is a lifelong pursuit. We grow in spiritual maturity moment by moment, day by day, year by year.

In many ways, spiritual exercise is a lot like physical exercise. If you stop exercising physically, your body may not show the results of inactivity for a while. But one day you wake up and find everything is sagging in all the wrong places.

—Jim George

3

Making Spiritual Growth Happen

Grow in the grace and knowledge of our Lord and Savior Jesus Christ.

—2 PETER 3:18

It's not hard for us to stir up the motivation to do the things that we *want* to do, is it? While we may find it hard to get excited about making repairs around the house or going to work in the morning, we are usually energetic and enthused when it comes to enjoying a personal hobby or taking time for recreation.

Now, the activities that people are motivated to be involved in can be positive, or they can be negative. For instance, where I live in Washington I can look out my window overlooking a lake and spot men in their boats—as early as 5:00 A.M.—fishing in the lake. Some of them are still on the lake after 5:00 P.M., staying until the sun sets. Some of the men are infrequent visitors, but others come to the lake again and again, but never with their families. I honestly can't help but wonder about their family life. Are they married? If so, how could these husbands possibly spend any time with their wives if they're always fishing? And how about their children? I constantly hear from dads bemoaning the woes of getting along with their teenagers, and in the back of my mind, I wonder if some of these dads have even made an effort to relate to their children.

I don't say this in criticism of fishing, but rather, to point out that the things we enjoy need to be kept in the context of the priorities God has set for life. The things that motivate us—whether it be sports, fishing, hiking, swimming, or whatever—can have a positive effect or negative effect depending on how we handle them. For example, I am a runner. I love to run, and because of the many beneficial side effects of running, I somehow, even with an overly full schedule, still manage to get out on the road and run. I do so because I really want to—and, as I said, we do what we want to do. The key is making sure we don't neglect other important elements in our lives as we pursue our interests.

So far in this book we've considered others and the nature of their heart and their desires. As Christians, it should be natural for us to *want* to grow spiritually. As we saw earlier, David's heart eagerly desired to follow God, and so did John Wesley's. We'll soon spend time looking at what motivated the apostle Paul, and I even shared a bit about the desires of my own heart. But now it's time to look at your heart and desires. What is the burning desire of your soul? My hope is that you're saying, "I want to be a man after God's own heart. I want to grow spiritually. I want my life to have a positive spiritual impact on others. I want to be all God wants me to be. But *how* do I begin?"

This is a wonderful desire to have, and it will very definitely have a positive impact on your life and on everyone around you. What's exciting is that as you pursue this desire and see the positive results, you become motivated to even greater spiritual growth.

So, what are the steps to making this kind of growth happen? Let's look at them.

Steps for Pursuing Spiritual Growth

1. *Devote your life to Jesus Christ.* Have you already taken the step of receiving Jesus as the Savior and Lord of your life? As I said earlier, this is truly the first step in becoming a man after God's own heart. Once you become a Christian, the Holy Spirit comes into your life and works to fulfill God's will for your life. You, like Jesus' disciples, are ready to obey His command to "follow me" (Mark 1:17).

2. *Deal with sin.* Sin is any thought, word, or deed that goes against God's instructions in the Bible. And, my friend, sin will always inhibit your spiritual growth. Going back to David and his life, we can clearly see how sin can ruin a man and the effect it can have on his career and his family. For example, consider David's affair with Bathsheba. To cover up the fact that he had gotten Bathsheba pregnant, David had her husband killed in battle (1 Samuel 18). For one full year afterward, David kept silent about his sins. Read David's personal description of what happened to him during that year:

> When I kept silent, my bones wasted away through my groaning all day long. For day and night your hand was heavy upon me; my strength was sapped as in the heat of summer. Then I acknowledged my sin to you and did not cover up my iniquity. I said, "I will confess my transgressions to the LORD"—and you forgave the guilt of my sin (Psalm 32:3-5).

David experienced some very real physical side effects because of his sins—his body wasted away, he groaned from pain, his vitality was drained, his strength was sapped, his life was ebbing away. And the spiritual side effects must have been equally bad or even worse! David knew he had done wrong. And he knew he couldn't hide that from God.

Now, you may be thinking, *I'm not a major-league sinner like David. I haven't murdered anyone or had an affair. My sins are just little ones. My sins aren't hurting anyone.*

But Jesus put the seriousness of sin into perspective when He said that even if you merely get angry with someone, you have committed murder in your heart (Matthew 5:22). And even if you lust after a woman in your mind, you have committed adultery with her in your heart (Matthew 5:28).

The bottom line on sin is that any sin, whether big or small, whether overt or covert, is an affront to a holy God and must be confessed and forsaken. Friend, anytime you and I have unconfessed sin in our life, it will hurt our relationship with God and affect our spiritual growth, as well as affect our loved ones and our work.

Why not take a few moments now and reflect on your own life? Is there unconfessed sin? Do you need to acknowledge your sin to God as David did? As a man after God's own heart, David confessed his sin. He then experienced the wonderful cleansing that came with his confession and declared, "Blessed is he whose transgressions are forgiven, whose sins are covered" (Psalm 32:1).

If you want to experience the cleansing that comes with God's forgiveness and the freedom from guilt that is caused by sin, then you'll want to make it a habit to confess your sins to the Lord. When you do so, remember to thank God for His forgiveness...and then move on to greater growth!

3. *Discard spiritual laziness.* In years past, I was a part of a men's Saturday morning Bible study at my church. The study started at 7:00 A.M., so I had to leave home about 6:30 to get

there on time. Each Saturday as I drove to the church, my route took me by a golf course that was filled with men playing golf. Because many were already far along on the golf course, it was evident they had gotten there much earlier in the morning. These guys had to have gotten there at six in the morning!

Then I would arrive at church, where just a few men would show up to study God's Word. I was always amazed that so many non-Christian men could get up so early on Saturday morning to play golf, but so few Christian men would be willing to get up early to study and grow in God's Word. Now, there's nothing wrong with playing golf early on Saturday. My point is that if you're failing to set aside some time for God in your life and instead choosing to spend that time on your own pleasures, then you're hurting your spiritual growth.

I know this is not an easy matter, for I'm constantly having to evaluate my choices. What we need to ask ourselves is this: Am I choosing the world over God and His Word? Am I choosing worldly hobbies and sports to the point of excluding time spent in the study of God's Word with God's men?

Why not invite the Lord to help you with your choices? Why not determine to spend more time with God in His Word, and more time with other men of God studying His Word? Why not begin a spiritual exercise program and firm up your spiritual muscles? That's what being a man after God's own heart is all about.

4. *Decide the method of growth.* What's wonderful about starting a spiritual exercise program is that there are many great tools available to help you grow. Depending on your work schedule, lifestyle, and responsibilities, different types of study helps are available. You may want to start with resources that help you study the Bible by yourself. To assist you in your personal study, I have included, in the back of the book, some practical tips on how to study the Bible (see pages 245-50). Or

you may want to get involved in a group Bible study program with other men who also desire to grow.

Here are some additional possibilities:

- Listen to the Bible on audiotape, or to audiotapes of your favorite preacher
- View sermons or classroom lectures on videotape
- Attend night classes to study books of the Bible, Christian living, theology, and so on
- Start memorizing key Scripture verses
- Utilize a combination of some of these or other suggestions

Above all, you'll want to read through your Bible on a regular basis. God's Word will always be your main source of spiritual nourishment. I once heard a startling statistic that reported that less than five percent of all Christians have read through their Bible even once. That means the simple practice of reading the Bible regularly will put you in the top percentile of all Christians—and to read the entire Bible in one year takes only about five to ten minutes a day!

Friend, determining to read through your Bible is a decision you must make. Your pastor can't make it for you. Your wife or a friend can't make it for you. No, you must decide! And to help you do that, I've placed a Bible reading schedule in the back of this book. You'll want to make a commitment to read the Bible daily, which will help you in your pursuit of spiritual growth. You may also want to ask someone else to hold you to that commitment. You'll discover that sharing about your spiritual growth with a friend will provide you with a wonderful source of encouragement and support.

5. *Determine to be discipled.* If we want to grow, it's necessary for us to be learners. One of the best ways to learn is to find someone who can help lead you upward and onward to spiritual maturity. That's what it means to be discipled, or mentored.

Every man who wants to be a man after God's own heart will benefit from having a role model who can help provide counsel, guidance, and encouragement on a regular basis. When I was a young Christian, I knew I needed help. Did I ever! I had a wife and two little girls, and, quite frankly, I didn't have a clue about what I should be doing. So I looked for someone who was further along in his spiritual growth to assist me in mine. I can only thank God that I didn't have far to go—there were several godly men in my church who could come alongside me and help.

Over the years I've met with many different men who have helped me to mature. I owe them a tremendous debt! And eventually I grew to the point where I could also start meeting with spiritually younger men and sharing with them what I had learned.

The Bible strongly encourages men like you and me to be involved in such discipleship. Paul exhorted one of his disciples in this way: "The things you have heard me say in the presence of many witnesses entrust to reliable men who will also be qualified to teach others" (2 Timothy 2:2).

This verse brings to mind a relay race. Paul spoke these words to Timothy, his disciple, who was to take the baton of God's truth and pass it on to other faithful men. These faithful men were then to pass that baton of truth on to others, who were then to pass it on to still others. This spiritual relay race has continued down through the centuries, and now the baton is being handed to you and me! Brother, we must take hold of that baton and make sure we pass it on to others. The race, humanly speaking, depends on us passing that baton faithfully and successfully. Let's not fail the Lord in our assignment!

6. *Dedicate your life to ongoing spiritual growth.* Spiritual growth is a lifelong pursuit. We grow in spiritual maturity moment by moment, day by day, year by year. In many ways, spiritual exercise is a lot like physical exercise. If you stop exercising physically, your body may not show the results of inactivity for a while. But one day you will wake up and find everything is sagging in all the wrong places. (That happened to me at about age 35!)

In the same way, you may think you can get by without reading the Bible, praying, and being discipled. One day, however, you'll wake up and find yourself spiritually flabby and out of shape...all because you didn't make a focused effort to keep growing day by day. And remember, you can't rest on yesterday's growth. You must be dedicated to growing today and every day.

The Benefits of Spiritual Growth

As you consider the steps involved in making spiritual growth possible, are you thinking, *This isn't at all easy!* While it's true that growth involves action on your part, the benefits of such growth are phenomenal and well worthwhile. Here's what happens when you become a man after God's own heart:

- You will enjoy greater intimacy with God
- You will manifest Christlike behavior to a watching world
- You will be able to give your family the spiritual leadership they need
- You will possess the spiritual strength needed to defend against temptation

- You will provide a model of spiritual strength and maturity for other men
- You will have the spiritual resources to disciple others

We started this chapter talking about motivation and desire. And I have to tell you that the very fact that we can enjoy these kinds of benefits and blessings motivates me, by the grace of God, to *keep* on becoming a man after God's own heart! I'm praying the same is true for you.

Give Me a Man of God

Give me a man of God—one man,
Whose faith is master of his mind,
And I will right all wrongs
And bless the name of all mankind.

Give me a man of God—one man,
Whose tongue is touched with heaven's fire,
And I will flame the darkest hearts
With high resolve and clean desire.

Give me a man of God—one man,
One mighty prophet of the Lord,
And I will give you peace on earth,
Bought with a prayer and not a sword.

Give me a man of God—one man,
True to the vision that he sees,
And I will build your broken shrines
And bring the nations to their knees.[6]

I have read the lives of many eminent Christians who have been on earth since the Bible days. Some of them, I see, were rich, and some poor. Some were learned, some unlearned. Some of them were Episcopalians, and some Christians of other denominations. Some were Calvinists, and some were Arminians. Some have loved to use a liturgy, and some chose to use none. But one thing, I see, they all had in common. They all have been men of prayer.[7]

—J. C. Ryle

4

The Marks of a Man After God's Own Heart

Part I

Very early in the morning, while it was still dark, Jesus got up, left the house, and went off to a solitary place, where he prayed.

—Mark 1:35

Before I joined the pastoral staff at Grace Community Church in Sun Valley, California, I had spent my career in the pharmaceutical industry. Why pharmacy? Perhaps because in my small hometown, the first job I ever had was in the local drugstore. I swept the floor, stocked the shelves, and worked as a general "delivery boy." I liked the environment—it was clean, it was busy with people, and it was all about helping others to get well. And my boss, a strong Christian, made the atmosphere a stimulating and enjoyable place to be. I liked it so much that I began taking the coursework that ultimately lead to graduating from the University of Oklahoma School of Pharmacy.

Since graduation, I've been in and out of the medical field for more than 35 years. I've worked as a pharmacist in drugstores and hospitals, and, after entering the ministry, I continued on with the Medical Service Corps of the Army reserves. To this day, I still keep my pharmacy license current. To do that, I must complete a certain number of hours of continuing education throughout the year.

To maintain my pharmacy license, I'm required to understand how various drugs work, and what they can and cannot be used for. This means a pharmacist can be confident that each class or group of drugs has its own consistent unique set of actions and reactions. These characteristics, or marks, are common for all medications in that class. This makes it possible to know that certain drugs, when used, will obtain certain results. If drugs didn't have consistent characteristics, we wouldn't be able to make reliable use of them.

A Heart That Obeys

Are you wondering what all of this has to do with being a man after God's own heart? Well, just as classes of medicine have similar characteristics, so, too, do men after God's own heart. In other words, every man after God's own heart will share some similar traits. And so far, we've considered the bottom-line mark of God's man. Did you catch it? *A man after God's own heart is a man who yearns to please God, a man who nurtures a heart that obeys.*

This was true of David. In our previous chapter we discovered that David was a man after God's own heart because he desired to do all God's will (Acts 13:22). This was true for David, and friend, it's also true for any man who desires to be a man after God's own heart. It's crucial that we know God's will...and obey it! Yes, this is a rather simplistic way of looking at all that's involved in true spiritual growth, but basically that's the key to being God's man—knowing God's Word and obeying it. As I said, this characteristic or mark ultimately is the bottom-line mark of God's man.

I know I've shared this already, but in my own life I've been extremely blessed to have some men who belong to "the honorable class of men after God's own heart" as personal mentors through the years. It is in these friendships that some additional marks of godliness became evident to me. As I observed the lives of these godly men "up close and personal," I began to realize that the marks of the godly men in the Bible (men like Moses, Joseph, Nehemiah, Paul, and, of course, David) are the same marks evident in all godly men.

With that in mind, what are some of the other marks of a man after God's own heart? What are other qualities that set such a man apart, whether it's a man who lived 3,000 years ago, or a man—like you and me—living today? We've already seen in Acts 13:22 that such a man desires to obey God. Let's look at one more primary mark here, and then we'll look at several more characteristics in the next chapter.

A Heart That Prays

When you read through the Bible, it becomes clear that men who desired God were men of prayer. These few examples give us an idea of the importance of prayer as a trait in the lives of men who were used by God:

- *Abraham,* throughout his life, built altars and called upon the name of the Lord (Genesis12:7-8).
- *Moses* was constantly on his knees praying for God's direction as he led the nation of Israel (Exodus 34:12-16).
- *David* prayed for forgiveness for his foolish decision to number the people under his rule (2 Samuel 24:10).

- *Solomon,* the great king of Israel, prayed for wisdom in order to judge the nation rightly (1 Kings 3:9).
- *Daniel* prayed a prayer of confession for himself and on behalf of his people, asking God to return the Jews to their homeland (Daniel 9:3-19).
- *Nehemiah* prayed for God's protection throughout the rebuilding of Jerusalem's wall (Nehemiah 4:9).
- *The apostles* prayed for guidance after the ascension of Jesus (Acts 1:14).
- *The apostle Paul* prayed constantly for the churches where he had ministered (2 Corinthians 11:28). He was also in continuous prayer for the men he had discipled (2 Timothy 1:2-3).

Paul, when he wrote to Timothy about how the church at Ephesus should offer worship, said, "I urge, then, first of all, that requests, prayers, intercession and thanksgiving be made..." (1 Timothy 2:1). A bit later, Paul gave this exhortation: "I want the men everywhere to lift up holy hands in prayer" (verse 8). Paul saw prayer as a primary ministry of the church, and he wanted the men in the church to be active in this important function of worship.

Maybe you're already enjoying a meaningful prayer life. But if you're like most of us, there's probably room for improvement—maybe even *lots* of room! The biggest problem for me is that it's easy to let other things crowd out most of my opportunities for prayer. Perhaps you can identify with that problem, too. J. Oswald Sanders, a widely loved and respected Bible teacher and author, said it well when he stated:

> Mastering the art of prayer, like any other art, will take time, and the amount of time we

allocate to it will be the true measure of our conception of its importance.[8]

So...what will it take for you and me to master the art of prayer, to develop a heart that prays?

Time—Obviously, *time* is a key element in developing a vital prayer life. If you and I want to be men after God's own heart, we need to set aside a time during the day to develop the art of and a heart for prayer. For me, the best time for prayer is early in the morning. I'm more likely to pray if I include it in my early morning quiet time along with my Bible reading.

On many occasions (and I know this probably won't sound very spiritual) I pray as I go running. I take my prayer list in hand...or in my heart...and start running. As I begin pounding the pavement and praying, I seem to lose myself in prayer (and, as an added benefit, the pain of the jog is forgotten!).

For you, there may be other times of the day that are more appropriate for prayer. But as J. Oswald Sanders said a moment ago, the amount of time we give to something indicates its importance to us. So let's give prayer the time that it requires and deserves. After all, it's a mark—a vibrant mark—of a man after God's own heart.

Place—Next we need a *place* where we can commune with God. That place, like mine often is, might be out on an open road or on a bike path while you're running. Or it might be in a quiet place at home before the family gets up. Many men have told me that the best time and place for them to pray is in the car while commuting to work. You don't have to be in a closet with your eyes closed to talk to God about the issues and desires of your life. Rather than listen to the radio or CDs or think about last night's sports scores, you can focus on God in your car and lift your prayer to Him. In a spirit of worship, you can recite and meditate on Scripture. And you can pray, talking to God about what's on your heart.

Jesus Christ is our perfect example of a man of prayer. Throughout the Gospels we see Jesus taking time to pray to the Father for strength and guidance for His life. In Mark 1:35 we read about the fact that He set aside both a *time* and a *place:* "Very *early in the morning*, while it was still dark, Jesus got up, left the house and went off to a *solitary place*, where he prayed" (emphases added).

Pattern—Third, we need a *pattern* after which we can build a life of prayer. How did you learn any skill that's now a part of your life? How did you learn to catch a ball, to ride a bicycle, to drive a car? You learned by *doing*. So it is with prayer—we learn to pray by praying. There's no shortcut. The more regularly you pray, the more of a habit it becomes, and the more skilled you become. Then, over time, you'll gain a greater sensitivity as to how you can pray more effectively. Also, the more regularly you come to God in prayer, the more aware you'll become of His presence...and your sin. Both of these awarenesses will help you in becoming a man after God's own heart.

Lifestyle—The Bible calls us to a *lifestyle* or attitude of constant prayer. We are commanded to "pray continually" (1 Thessalonians 5:17). And because we have the Spirit of God living in us, and because He knows what we should be praying for (Romans 8:26-27), we can be purposefully praying at all times, in every place, by any pattern, as a lifestyle. Brother, such a lifestyle of prayer is a distinct mark of a man after God's own heart.

And speaking of prayer, I'm praying that our discussion about prayer has made you hunger to have this mark of godly character become more prominent in your life. That is what's been tugging on my own heart as I've been writing about it. (In fact, I'm resisting the urge to tie on my tennis shoes and hit the road so that I can spend some quality time praying...because I want to try to finish this chapter first!) And before we close, here are a few time-honored suggestions on how we can begin to develop a more consistent pattern of prayer in our lives:

- Start where you are. For me, whenever I am out of the habit of praying, I start with just a few minutes each day.
- Start with your priorities. Pray for your own spiritual growth first. Then, if you're married and have children, pray for your family. Pray to be God's man in your home and in your family relationships.
- Start with a prayer list. Take a three-by-five card and jot down those people and issues that are important to you and to God. Then pray faithfully for these people and issues. (What's great about using a card is that you can tuck it into your shirt pocket all day long, prop it up against your computer, hold it in your hand as you drive the car, or, like me, as you run.)
- Start developing a pattern of praying—one day at a time.
- Start asking God for wisdom on how to pray (Romans 8:26-27).
- Start reaping the blessings of answered prayer.

There it is, friend. Do you want to follow hard after God, to be His man, to affect the lives of others for good, for eternity? Then prayer is needed. And the side effect is wonderful—you'll start reaping the blessings of answered prayer. As friend and author Terry Glaspey remarks in his excellent book on prayer, "Prayer is, indeed, one of the most important factors in our spiritual growth. It can be said with absolute certainty that

Christians who pray are Christians who experience spiritual growth."[9]

Dear brother, the marks of a man after God's own heart go on...and so will we, in the next chapter. But let's briefly sum up what we've learned so far about becoming a man after God's own heart. We've seen that a man after God's own heart possesses...

- a heart that is saved,
- a heart for God's Word,
- a heart that obeys,
- a heart that prays.

Won't you take a moment to pray that yours is such a heart?

Wanted—a Man!

What we lack and sorely need,
For want of which we bleed, and bleed,
Is men of a more godly breed...
Honest men in highest places;
Men with single aims and faces;
Men whose nobler thought outpaces
Thought of self, or power, or pelf...
Men whose axes need no grinding;
Men who are not always minding
First their own concerns, and blinding
Their souls' eyes to larger things...
Men of wide and godly vision;
Men of quick and wise decision;
Men who shrink not at derision...
Men whose souls have wings.[10]

Theodore Roosevelt said,
"You may worship God anywhere at any time. But the chances are that you will not do so unless you have first learned to worship him in some particular place at some particular time." [11]

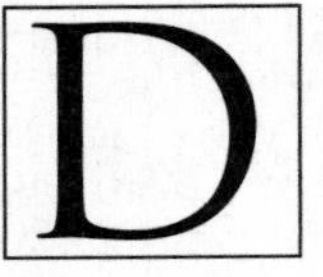

avid said,
"I rejoiced with those who said unto me, Let us go to the house of the LORD."

—PSALM 122:1

5

The Marks of a Man After God's Own Heart

Part II

God is spirit, and his worshipers must worship in spirit and in truth.

—JOHN 4:24

What can you and I do to develop the marks of a man after God's own heart? That's the question we've been addressing. I promised you a list of godly characteristics that we as men who desire to be godly and who desire a strong relationship with God can seek to develop. We began that list in the previous chapter, and so far we've looked at two of these marks—a heart that obeys God, and a heart that prays.

Now we're going to look at several more marks. And keep in mind as you're reading that there are certainly more that you and I could list. But the few marks I've chosen to mention here are among the most vital for stimulating us to get started in our pursuit to follow after God.

A Heart That Praises

What usually comes to mind when you think about David? If you're like me, you tend to think about David's "macho" achievements. He fought a lion and a bear. He felled a giant. He was a mighty man of war, conquering many foes. He was a great leader of men. He was a builder who established the "city of David." He was feared by his enemies. He was one of the greatest kings of the ancient world. There's no doubt David was a man's man, a leader's leader, and a warrior's warrior.

And yet David was a man with a tender heart toward God. He was a man who was constantly praising his God. He even characterized himself as "Israel's singer of songs," saying "[God's] word was on my tongue." David was one whom "the Spirit of the LORD spoke through" (2 Samuel 23:1-2).

David may not have always done things right, but God was never far from his thoughts. He knew the "secret" of his success. On one occasion David came before the Lord and voiced his utter amazement at God's blessing with these words: "Who am I, O Sovereign LORD, and what is my family, that you have brought me this far?" (2 Samuel 7:18). David couldn't help but break forth in praise!

Let's read through just a few of the many verses of praise penned by David. And as you read, think about how God has blessed you. Do you have a dear wife, loving children, a good church, a steady job, a place to live? If so, you have much to praise God for. And if some things are missing in your life, don't fail to praise God anyhow. Your loving and all-knowing God knows where you are and what you need. Therefore you can praise Him for His wisdom. (I hope you're catching on to the need and the simplicity of developing a heart that praises the Lord.)

Again, let's consider David's example:

> I will give thanks to the LORD...and will sing praise to the name of the LORD Most High (Psalm 7:17).
>
> Sing to the LORD, you saints of his; praise his holy name (Psalm 30:4).
>
> Sing joyfully to the LORD, you righteous; it is fitting for the upright to praise him (Psalm 33:1).
>
> I will extol the LORD at all times; his praise will always be on my lips (Psalm 34:1).

David sets a good example for us, doesn't he? He shows us that a man after God's own heart is a man who is not afraid to verbalize his love for God. He openly and constantly practiced the presence of God. David's heart uttered praise upon praise throughout his day. Again, God was never far from his thoughts—wherever David was, he took the opportunity to worship his God.

So you too, as a man who loves God, should not hesitate in the least to praise God. Whether while working in an office, driving out on the freeway, or relaxing at home with your family, you as God's man should want to continually offer up praise to God in your heart and with your lips (Hebrews 13:15).

How can you practice the presence of God? Here are some suggestions that have been helpful to me in offering praise to the Lord:

Meditate on God's power—I rarely go through a day without thinking of Paul's meditation on God's strength: "I can do everything through him who gives me strength" (Philippians 4:13). Do you have a problem today—a challenge you are facing, a problem at work that you must resolve, an issue with your wife or a child or someone else? Then help yourself to

God's power available to you through this one mighty truth...and turn your gratitude for God's power into praise.

Memorize psalms of praise—I especially love Psalm 118:24: "This is the day the LORD has made; let us rejoice and be glad in it." It's another "attitude lifter," so to speak. As I square off with each new day (and its challenges), this one verse from just one of the 150 psalms puts a fresh spin on the day! Try it, use it, and memorize it. God's Word is powerful—powerful enough to transform any hesitation to praise.

Master God's promises—Estimates on the number of promises in the Bible vary from 7,487 to 30,000.[12] I urge you to pick one. *Any* one! Again (maybe because I'm under the pressure of a book deadline), I look to the promises of God each day to help me—promises such as this one: "Praise be to the LORD, to God our Savior, who daily bears our burdens" (Psalm 68:19). Friend, help yourself to this promise and see what happens to your burdens. I know you'll sense renewed confidence and comfort.

Marvel over God's provisions—Paul boldly declared, "My God will meet all your needs according to his glorious riches in Christ Jesus" (Philippians 4:19). What a wonderful God we have! He is going to provide for all our needs, not *out of* the riches of our Savior, but *according to* His riches. Do you see the difference? You and I have much to praise God for as we experience His glorious provision minute by minute and day by day for all of eternity.

Mull over God's presence—As David thought about the fact of God's presence, He expressed his awe with these words: "Where can I go from your Spirit? Where can I flee from your presence?" (Psalm 139:7). We can almost sense the exclamation marks after these thoughts. The answers to David's rhetorical questions are an obvious "Nowhere!" Think about it: It doesn't matter where you go—God is there. It doesn't matter what's happening when you get there—God is there.

To know that God is with you everywhere should be comforting. To know that God is with your family at all times should be equally comforting. Do you praise and thank Him for His constant presence? David truly understood the reality of God's presence and practiced it when he stated, "I have set the LORD always before me. Because he is at my right hand, I will not be shaken" (Psalm 16:8). Mulling over God's presence should cause us to have confidence in Him...and to praise Him.

Magnify on God's Protection—King Saul, David's predecessor to the throne (and also his father-in-law!), repeatedly tried to kill David. So, for much of his young adulthood, David had to exercise caution or even flee from town because of these death threats. Yet even in those circumstances, David could pen this well-known verse: "Even though I walk through the valley of the shadow of death, I will fear no evil, for you are with me" (Psalm 23:4). What peace is ours when we understand that we are under God's protective hand! The next time you sense fear, practice the presence of God and "fear no evil," for God is with you. Now *that's* praiseworthy!

Friend, as you and I practice the presence of God in these ways, we will be tremendously blessed. And so will every person we come in contact with. They, too, will be affected and blessed by our hearts of praise. This positive, God-centered spirit of praise will make people want that same spirit. Why not, just for today, try putting Psalm 34:1 into practice: "His praise will always be on my lips"? I believe you'll see a difference in your attitude toward your day. And I know that others, as a result, will have a different attitude toward you and your God.

A Heart That Worships

Up to now we've been talking about the *personal* side of worship as we've described the marks of a man after God's heart. God's man is marked by prayer, praise, and personal worship. As he reads, memorizes, and meditates on God's Word, he develops a deep reservoir of strength that, in time, issues forth in praise and prayers of gratitude for his God.

But there is another aspect of worship—the *public* side. From the very beginnings of the church, believers have gathered together to worship God through singing, studying the Word, and celebrating the Lord's resurrection. In fact, the day the early church gathered together was called "the first day of the week" or "the Lord's Day" (Acts 20:7; Revelation 1:10).

On calendars, Sunday is the first day of the week. And for Christians, there are several reasons it is an important day. Hear what my friend and author Dr. Richard Mayhue of The Master's Seminary believes are good reasons for us as men after God's heart to participate in corporate worship:

- It provides the only opportunity during the week for the entire flock to hear the heart, mind, and voice of the Senior Shepherd.
- It's the only day during the week for God's flock to join their hearts together in unified worship.
- It's the only time during the week that the flock can blend their voices together in praise to God.
- It's the only time during the week to join hands in giving sacrificially to the Lord.
- It's the only opportunity during the week in which the congregation (both young and old) can have a common shared experience.

- It's the only time during the week in which the large body can be in a position to encourage and stimulate one another to love and good deeds in accord with Hebrews 10:24-25.[13]

You and I—as men aspiring to godliness—should be as excited about going to church as David was about his visits to the house of God. Hear again how David, a man who had a heart for worship, expressed his yearning for God's house. This longing ought to be ours as well:

> I love the house where you live, O LORD, the place where your glory dwells (Psalm 26:8).

> One thing I ask of the LORD, this is what I seek: that I may dwell in the house of the LORD all the days of my life, to gaze upon the beauty of the LORD and to seek him in his temple (Psalm 27:4).

An additional (and I might add, important) reason church attendance is important is your family. Your wife and children need spiritual stimulation as much as you do! Therefore you must take leadership in this vital area. It's not your wife's responsibility to make church attendance happen. It's *your* responsibility as a husband and father and the God-ordained spiritual leader of your family. God holds *you* accountable for nurturing your family's spiritual needs, and church attendance is a key part of that nurturing.

In fact, Sunday worship should be the highlight of your week. You and your family should look forward to Sunday with anticipation, and use the weekdays preparing yourselves for worshiping God with His people in His house.

A Heart That Serves

Several months ago I had dinner with a man who was a deacon in his church. With great energy he told me about how he loved to serve the people at his church. He was so enthusiastic that he gestured a lot as he spoke, and I became a little embarrassed because we were in a packed restaurant. Yet nothing could keep this man's excitement down as he continued to tell me of his passion for serving God. He constantly looked for opportunities throughout the week to serve the needs of fellow church members, and on Sunday he couldn't wait to get to church so he could continue his ministry of service. This man's zeal for service may seem excessive at first glance, but in actuality, he was exhibiting yet another mark of a man after God's heart—a heart that yearns to serve.

As fleshly humans, our natural (and selfish) tendency is to take care of our own needs first. We like to make sure there is plenty of time for the things we want to do. Then if we have any time or energy left over, we might be willing to use it to serve someone else.

But as men after God's own heart, you and I need to resist these selfish tendencies and strive instead to see ourselves as servants. In fact, in the Bible, we see many of the great men in the Old Testament described as servants. God spoke of Abraham as His servant (Genesis 26:24). Joshua was called "the servant of the LORD" at his death (Joshua 24:29). And David, too, was called "my servant" by God (2 Samuel 7:5). In the New Testament we see that godly men were chosen by the church in Jerusalem to serve the physical needs of the widows (Acts 6:1-6). And the apostle Paul referred to himself as a servant of God (Romans 1:1).

The Lord Jesus Christ is, of course, our supreme example. He is our model of what it means to be a servant. Jesus said of

Himself, "the Son of Man did not come to *be* served, but *to* serve" (Matthew 20:28, emphases added).

Read through these verses about Jesus and think about any changes you need to make in your life so that you, like Jesus, can better assume the role of a servant. As you cultivate a servant heart, you'll find yourself wanting to love and serve your family, your church, and others. I've altered the format of these verses (Philippians 2:3-8) so that the various elements of a servant's heart are more obvious:

> Do nothing out of selfish ambition or vain conceit, but in humility consider others better than yourselves.
>
> Each of you should look not only to your own interests, but also to the interests of others.
> Your attitude should be the same as that of Christ Jesus:
>
> Who, being in very nature God,
> did not consider equality with God something to be grasped, but made himself nothing,
>
> taking the very nature of a servant,
> being made in human likeness.
>
> And being found in appearance as a man,
> he humbled himself and became obedient to death—even death on a cross!

Over the last two chapters, we've looked at five of the marks of a man after God's own heart. There are other marks, too, but these are some of the most foundational ones—obedience, prayer, praise, worship, and service. The reason I wanted us to focus on these five marks in particular is because our goal in the upcoming chapters will be to see how these marks are "fleshed out" in everyday life...as we live out the priorities God has set for a man after His own heart. With that in mind, won't you join me for a brief moment of prayer?

> Lord, my heartfelt cry is that as other men look at my life, they would see the life of Jesus shining forth through me. Work in my life and make me one of your "marked" men. And when others see these marks, may they desire godliness in their lives and want to follow You as well. I pray that I will…

…obey Your Word without question,
…pray without ceasing,
…praise You constantly,
…worship You continuously,
…and serve others unconditionally.

Part Two

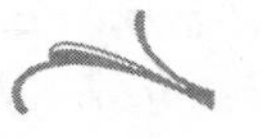

The Pursuit of God's Priorities

Husband, as you seek to obey God, pray that He will work His kind of love in you. Plan and carry out ways to show biblical love to your wife and most likely she will respond with great enthusiasm.[14]

—Stuart Scott

6
A Heart That Loves Your Wife
Part I

Husbands, love your wives,
just as Christ loved the church
and gave Himself up for her...

—Ephesians 5:25

As a minister, I've officiated at my share of weddings over the decades, including the weddings of both my daughters. And recently I was asked by one of my former students from The Master's Seminary to perform his wedding ceremony. It's always a special privilege and honor to be asked to participate in anyone's wedding, but in this case, the request was especially exciting for several reasons.

First, Brian had been involved in youth work and missions since his high-school days, so he hadn't had much time for dating. At the time he became engaged to Anita, he was entering his thirties! Second, Brian is now the pastor of a wonderful church in faraway South Africa. I had visited South Africa in past years when I conducted leadership conferences, but my visits had always been during the summer, which meant in South Africa, it was winter. Even in their "winter," South Africa is one of the most beautiful countries I've ever visited. However, to my good fortune, Brian and Anita's wedding was to be held in November, which meant my first "summer" visit, not to mention an opportunity to expose my wife, Elizabeth, to this beautiful country for the first time.

The wedding ceremony was held in a quaint, open chapel outside of Johannesburg. The summer flowers were in full bloom, and the temperature was mild because we were at 5,000 feet above sea level. The bride and groom stood before me in traditional wedding attire as I spoke to everyone about the nature of Christian love.

Because I happened to be writing this book during the months Brian and I planned my part in the wedding, I had the opportunity to reflect on what it really means for a husband to love his wife. As I thought through the vows this prize couple would share with each other, I reminisced about my own vows spoken over 36 years earlier.

Remembering Your Wedding

To be honest, I can't remember much about my wedding or what was said during the ceremony—it's all a blur in my mind. I do, however, remember coming into the church from a side entrance with the minister and my best man. There I stood, in front of all those people, waiting for my bride-to-be...with a beet-red face! No, I wasn't embarrassed or suffering from an attack of hives. I was sunburned from water-skiing all day with my buddies from the wedding party! The wedding started at 8:00 P.M., and it must have been an extremely short ceremony, because in our after-wedding pictures my watch reads 8:20 P.M.!

Now let's put you on the hot spot. What about you and your wedding? In the months or years since that day, have you thought back on the vows you made to your bride? When was the last time you thought about your vows and the commitments you made? Are you like me, and can't remember a thing? I'm sure, if you're like most men, the last time you thought about the wedding ceremony was on the day of your wedding.

What's ironic about our tendency to forget about our vows is that our wedding day is one of the most important occasions in our life. What we say at that ceremony affects us for the rest of our lives. On that day, we vowed to love our wives "in sickness and health, in plenty and want, until death do us part." (I've got these vows memorized by now after so many weddings!) These promises were made not only before a church full of witnesses, but more importantly, before God.

I'm sure your vows were not idle words. You sincerely meant every promise you made to your bride on that day. But things don't always turn out the way we think they will. Most marriages, including mine, and I'm sure yours as well, have their "bumps" along the way. Hopefully we've weathered these bumps and are now on some smooth road.

The issue, however, is not the past. The past is over. We must leave the past and move on. It was the apostle Paul who said, "One thing I do: Forgetting what is behind and straining toward what is ahead, I press on..." (Philippians 3:13-14). We must press on. Yes, we can and should learn from the past. But what's more important is for us to think about what we can do *today* and *every day* in the future to truly fulfill the vows we made to our bride—whether those vows were made yesterday, last week, last year, or in my case, 36 years ago.

What *should* our wedding vows mean to us today? And what *does* it mean to love our wife?

Loving Your Wife

You may have heard the story about the man and woman who were having marital problems after 15 years of marriage and went to a counselor. In the middle of the session, the wife complained to the counselor, "He never tells me he loves me anymore." The man gave a surprised look and responded with, "Well, I told her I loved her when we got married, and it still stands." That's a long time for him to go without expressing his love for her (at least he remembered something from his wedding vows!).

I'm sure you would never be as insensitive as this man was to the need to verbally express his love to his wife. At the same time, however, it's always good for us to be reminded of the nature of true biblical love and how it is expressed. That's because we as husbands are called to display this kind of love to our wives daily. For our refresher course, let's go to the book of Ephesians.

Looking at the Supreme Example of Love

In the previous chapter, I quoted Paul's description of Jesus Christ as the perfect example of a sacrificial servant (Philippians 2:3-8). We learned that Christ served others even to the point of death. And Jesus is also our supreme example when it comes to love. In Ephesians 5:22-33 Paul points out five ways Jesus demonstrates His love for those of us who make up His church. And friend, in the same way Jesus loved the church, you and I are to love our wives. Read Ephesians 5:22-33, and then let's see what we can learn from Jesus' example.

The Specifics of Christ's Love

1. *Christ's love is a sacrificial love*—"Christ loved the church and gave himself up for her" (verse 25). Paul also spoke of this sacrifice for the church in Acts 20:28, where he reminds us that Christ purchased the church "with his own blood." As you can see, sacrificial love is costly!

Jesus' sacrifice is the perfect example of what love *demands*.

2. *Christ's love is a purifying love*—Regarding the church, Christ's goal was "to make her holy, cleansing her by the washing with water through the word, and to present her to himself as a radiant church, without stain or wrinkle or any other blemish, but holy and blameless" (verses 26-27). Jesus' love for the church seeks her purity and for her to be clothed in His holiness.

Jesus' love is the perfect example of what love *does*.

3. *Christ's love is a nurturing love*—"In this same way, husbands ought to love their wives as their own bodies. He who loves his wife loves himself. After all, no one ever hated his own body, but he feeds and cares for it, just as Christ does the church" (verses 28-29). Just as a man is concerned for the well-being of his own body, Jesus is concerned for the well-being of His body, the church. He tenderly cherishes her as something fragile, something precious, something very special.

Jesus' love is the perfect example of what love *develops*.

4. *Christ's love is an enduring love*—In familiar words frequently cited at weddings, Paul quotes from the Old Testament: "For this reason a man will leave his father and mother and be united to his wife, and the two will become one flesh" (verse 31). Commenting on this teaching, Paul explains, "This is a profound mystery—but I am talking about Christ and the church" (verses 32). Paul is telling us that our union with our wife is to be as lasting as Christ's union with His church. His is an everlasting love... regardless of how we act. Jesus' love is enduring and unconditional.

Jesus' love is the perfect example of love's *dedication*.

5. *Christ's love is an active love*—This statement summarizes all we've learned about biblical love, as exemplified by

Jesus. Perhaps it serves us as a summary statement. Jesus' love is the perfect example of love *demonstrated.*

True biblical love is sacrificing, purifying, nurturing, and enduring. This, my friend, is what it means to love your wife! Your love as a Christian husband has to go much farther and deeper than mere words and verbal expressions of love. The word translated "love" in Ephesians chapter 5 has little, if any, trace of usage in ancient writings outside of the Bible. It is a word born within the mind and heart of a truly loving God who demonstrated His love for us not by *saying* He loved us, but by *dying* for us! Now that's love in action! (And for that reason, both of us should be down on our knees in gratitude for the depth of God's love for us!)

Jesus' disciple John, sometimes called "the apostle of love," instructs us well on showing our love through actions. He writes, "Let us not love with words or tongue but with actions and in truth" (1 John 3:18).

Living Out Christ's Love

So what are some things you can do today to actively demonstrate a Christlike love to your dear wife? How can you live out His kind of love in your marriage? Let's take the elements of Jesus' love for the church one by one, and apply them to our marriages.

Sacrifice—This usually involves giving up something of yourself for someone else—such as your time, attention, or energy, and most of the time, this will mean going out of your way or enduring inconvenience. A marriage counselor put the concept of sacrifice in these words: "changing self-focused thoughts and actions to loving ones."[15] Thinking of your wife may mean large actions of sacrifice. But you can begin with a few smaller ones. Most of us say we would die for our wife, but we don't want to take out the trash! So let's start by taking care of the trash. And here are a few other ideas:

- Babysit the kids on a Saturday while your wife attends a woman's seminar at church or a woman's retreat (this is a no-brainer!).
- Make breakfast for the kids on Saturday morning and let your wife sleep in.
- Watch the kids one evening a week while your wife takes a Bible class at your church (better still—get a babysitter so both of you can take the class...then go out afterward and discuss the class over a cup of coffee).

Purity—Are you endeavoring to advance your wife's holiness? As Ephesians 5:26 teaches, you are to take every care that your wife is holy, clean, washed, "without stain or wrinkle or any other blemish, but holy and blameless." Are you catching on to God's message to you, friend? *You* must make sure you are endeavoring to be a holy example to your wife and encouraging her personal holiness. Do you want to know how? One practical way is to monitor your entertainment activities at home, including the TV programs and movies you watch. A godly man loves what is good and wholesome (Titus 1:8) and shuns what is not. *You* must set the highest example and the highest standards possible for you and your house, and desire that for your wife as well.

Nurture—To *nurture* means "to care for, develop, bring along, support, assist." What encouragement can you give your wife today in the things of God and in her spiritual advancement? In her efforts at managing the home? In her personal growth? Are there classes she can take to develop her gifts and abilities? Are there books you can give her that will put feet on her dreams and desires to be a godly woman? Is there a seminar coming up you could treat her to? Take an active role in assisting your wife's maturing process in the many facets of her life.

I've always encouraged Elizabeth to develop her God-given gifts and talents. And sometimes I did more than encourage—I pushed! Elizabeth's natural tendency is to be shy and to be by herself, and I've always thought she's had so many wonderful things to share with women. So I nudged her when she needed that extra nudge. And this ongoing support of my wife's desire to know and study the Bible has lead (thanks to God's grace) to her development as a women's Bible teacher and a writer. (And now, as I sit here writing this book, she's encouraging me!)

Endurance—As a runner, I can definitely tell you that there is a vast difference between a sprint...and a marathon! And marriage, of course, is not a sprint. It's a marathon! Your commitment to your marriage is not for a mere 100 yards. No, it's for an eternity (which is what running the 26 miles and 385 yards of a marathon must feel like!). Like a long-distance runner, you can't let yourself get discouraged about or distracted by the problems that come with everyday married life. And don't think that you can bail out because things aren't going your way. The permanent nature of your marriage vows means you need to "hunker down" for the long haul.

If you show your mate a love that sacrifices for her, purifies her, and nurtures her, you're likely to see your wife respond with great enthusiasm—and end up with a better marriage as a result. Then you'll find yourself enjoying the race, never wanting it to end. (Talk about a "runner's high"!)

Learning More About Love

I know we've covered a lot of territory in this chapter on loving our wives. Maybe the principles we've just learned seem a bit overwhelming at the moment. Let's see if we can make it easier by summing it all up in just two statements:

> Statement #1:
>
> *Jesus Christ is the supreme example of how to love*—He shows us how we as men after God's own heart should love our wives. How? In the same way that Jesus loved the church and gave Himself for her—with a sacrificial, purifying, nurturing, enduring love.
>
> Statement #2:
>
> *Love is active*—Telling your wife that you love her is important, but you and I both know that what's even more vital is our actions. We show our wives that we really do love them by our *works,* not just by our *words.*

Now the big question is this: What are some actions you and I can take to begin to communicate our love to our wives?

I'm glad you asked! In the next chapter, we're going to look at some very simple yet effective ways to say, "I love you." But first read the poem on the next page and ask yourself, "Could my wife have written these words to describe my love for her?"

Love

I love you...
not only for what you are,
but for what I am when I am with you.

I love you...
not only for what you have made of yourself,
but for what you are making of me.

I love you...
for the part of me that you bring out;

I love you...
for putting your hand into my heaped-up heart
and passing over all the foolish, weak things
that you can't help.
For dimly seeing there,
and for drawing out into the light
all the beautiful belongings
that no one else had looked
quite far enough to find.

I love you...
because you are helping me
to make of the lumber of my life
not a tavern but a temple;
out of the works of my every day
not a reproach but a song.[16]

en Keys to a Successful Marriage

Talk with each other.

Tell each other "I love you."

Touch each other.

Tantalize each other.

Tolerate each other.

Trust each other.

Treat each other.

Treasure each other.

Thank each other.

Track with each other.[17]

—KENNETH KILINSKI

7
A Heart That Loves Your Wife
Part II

He who finds a wife
finds what is good and
receives favor from the Lord.

—PROVERBS 18:22

As promised at the end of the previous chapter, we're going to look at some effective ways to truly demonstrate our love to our mates. What can you and I do to show our wives that our love is not just words—words glibly spoken at what seems like the appropriate moment? (And, if you really stop and think about it, the actions we're about to discuss were probably some of the very things you did to win your wife's affection in the first place!) Are you ready to remember what you did in the past to show your love, and to learn some new ideas as well? Every one of these guidelines can go far in strengthening your marriage.

Being Her Best Friend

Each of us has enjoyed one or more "best friends" over the years. I can remember my closest friends in high school. We did everything together. We vowed that we would never lose contact with each other, but...over time...our friendships waned...and died. Clearly, friends and friendships must be nurtured in order to stay alive. Absence does *not* necessarily make the heart grow fonder!

Let's go back to your courtship with your wife for a minute. Did you strive to be her best friend? I know you did! You were probably jealous if she spent time with any person other than you. Did you like being in her company and doing crazy things together? Elizabeth and I were the same way—we were best friends while we were dating.

During courtship, it seems as if the pure joy of just being together will never end. But after marriage, for some reason, that seems to fade away, doesn't it? What happened? Here's a basic formula that seems applicable to many of us:

time + familiarity + distractions + duties
= diminished interest

In other words, the demands and distractions of daily life crept into that beautiful friendship and began to erode the relationship.

How can you recapture that friendship you enjoyed with your wife while you two were dating? Think back on those days. What did you do to nurture your relationship with your wife-to-be? Take a moment to write a list. Then make a commitment to do some of these activities again—the activities that helped you to become best friends. After all, after your friendship with God, your wife's friendship is the greatest treasure you possess.

Spending Time Together

When you were dating your wife-to-be, how often did you want to be with her? If you were like me (and I'm sure you were), you wanted to be with her every waking minute. Do you still feel that way today? If the feelings aren't the same, then what happened in the intervening years? Have you grown so accustomed to your wife that you take her for granted? Would you rather be with the guys at a ball game? Or out fishing, or golfing? Or working late at the office? (Warning: Don't answer these questions!)

Most likely, because of your everyday obligations, the two of you aren't together much anyway. At most, you may have about an hour together in the morning before you—and maybe your wife, too—go to work. And in the evening, the two of you may have only two or three hours together before you both fall into bed after an exhausting day.

During those few hours—one in the morning and two or three in the evening—how much time do you really have alone, together, just the two of you? By the time you cook, eat, and clean up after a family meal, have a play time or homework time with the kids, get them all bathed and into bed, you and your wife may have only a few minutes of time alone.

Now, if you *do* have a few quality minutes that could be spent with your wife and you choose to do something else instead, you're making a statement (...and a mistake!). You're saying to your wife, "Someone or something else is more important than spending these few minutes with you."

I know you love your wife. And I know you're working on loving her as Christ loved the church. God has given you a beautiful and precious gift in your wife. That's what the Bible says—"He who finds a wife finds what is good and receives favor from the LORD" (Proverbs 18:22). If you've found a good wife, friend, you've found a treasure! That woman is a token of the Lord's favor to you. All I'm asking you to do is sit down with your wife-from-the-Lord, your treasure-gift from God, for a few minutes after work each day and ask her a few questions about her and her day. You'll be pleasantly surprised with the outcome! (And so will she!)

Going on a Date

You say you love your wife. You're starting to prove it by spending a few quality minutes together every day. Why not take your actions a step further and plan a time each week where it's just the two of you out on an old-fashioned date? How about dinner together? A drive? Something you both enjoy? Something that she enjoys…like maybe shopping (ugh!). Don't count the occasions when you're invited out or entertaining others. Also, don't let your children, business, a guest, or anything rob you of a weekly opportunity to show your wife you still love her and long to be with her.

Just imagine what one simple date a week (it doesn't have to be costly) could mean over the lifetime of a marriage. In 15 years that would mean 780 times you and your wife would have been together in-depth, 780 times you were alone without interruptions, 780 times when you were able to demonstrate your love to your wife. Don't you think such special times together would make a difference in your friendship?

I know it did for Elizabeth and me. And it doesn't have to be an expensive or elaborate date. For years our weekly date was hiring a babysitter for exactly two hours, walking across the street to a fast-food restaurant, and spending those two hours of time together talking, dreaming, listening to, and appreciating one another while we consumed two bottomless cups of coffee…for 89 cents!

Recently at a pastor's conference held at my former church, a pastor from the East Coast wanted to get together with me. But he had a problem—the only night I could meet with him was the same night he was babysitting for his host family so they could have their weekly date. I was very impressed that both the couple and this pastor—a guest—saw the importance of a "date night." No, we didn't meet…and I'm certain, as a result, something far greater was accomplished in that couple's marriage.

Friend, don't wait another week. Plan a date for this week. Again, you'll be pleasantly surprised with the outcome!

Being All There

The mind is an amazing thing. It can carry on *thousands* of functions at the same time! Sometimes that's good, and sometimes that's bad. For instance, when it thinks of someone or something else while your wife is talking to you...that's bad! There you are, looking right at your wife while she's pouring her heart out to you, and yet you're thinking about someone or something miles away.

What's even more amazing than the mind's capacity to wander is that your wife can tell when you're not listening! How does she do that?! We men think we are so clever. We nod at what we think is the right moment. We even make approving noises at obvious intervals. And yet our wives still catch us with our minds somewhere else!

When you're with your wife, especially if you're alone, the loving thing to do is to focus all your attention on her and be all there, both mentally and physically. This will take some concentration and effort on your part. For me, developing this kind of focused attention took some training. As a salesman I had to train myself to focus on the person I was trying to sell. And your wife is much more important than "making a sale"! Train yourself to devote your full attention on your wife when you are with her. The results of being all there will be better than any salesman could imagine!

Becoming a Better Listener

We're doing quite a bit of remembering, aren't we? Well, let's do it again. Remember back (again) to when you were dating your future wife. You hung on every word she spoke. You were an incredible listener! Why? Because you wanted to impress her. You wanted her to think you were the greatest guy on the planet. So what's changed? Shouldn't you still want her to think you are the greatest guy on the planet? Make the most of those very few precious opportunities when you are together and truly listen to what she is saying. Your wife will appreciate this more than you know! And especially listen when you have gone to all the trouble to plan a date together.

Communicating with your wife is important. One man put it this way: "The heart of marriage is its communication system. It can be said that the success and happiness of any married pair is measured in terms of the deepening dialogue which characterizes their union."[18]

I have to admit that listening hasn't been one of my better qualities as a husband! Too many times, I've excused myself by saying, "I've got so many responsibilities, so many obligations, so many pressures, I don't have time to really listen." (I'm sure you have your own set of excuses.) I've had to really work on becoming a better listener. Through the years, I've learned a few things about listening—things which I want to share with you now. These suggestions have been helpful to me, and you'll want to prayerfully consider making use of them so that you, too, might become a better listener:

- Realize that listening is an act of love. When you are listening, you are saying, "I value you as my wife and I want to hear what you have to say."
- Mentally remove your business hat and replace it with your husband's listening hat each day as you drive home from work. Try to think of specific questions to ask your wife about her day. These mental acts begin to prepare you to walk through the door and focus on your wife (as well as your family).

- Leave the briefcase at the office. (Or at least leave it in the car for a while!) The very act of leaving your work behind will help you to focus on your wife.
- Make it a priority when you arrive home to spend a few minutes asking your wife about her day. And doing this alone, over a cup of coffee or a soda, is even better!
- Stop what you're doing when your wife speaks to you. Look her in the eye and listen. This is what you do with everyone else, right? So why not do the same with your sweet wife?
- Ask questions as your wife talks. This helps you keep track of what she's saying.
- Think about how annoying it is when someone doesn't listen to *you*. That's how your *wife* feels when you fail to listen.

Renewing Your Vows

In this chapter we've been talking about loving our wife by our actions. I've given you four action steps you can use to demonstrate your love. And before we conclude, I would like to share with you one very significant way you can show your love for your wife.

Sit down with your wife in a quiet place, maybe on one of your upcoming date nights. Then, look her in the eye, and reaffirm your marriage vows to her. If you want, you can copy the following words and read them to your forever bride:

I, (your name), take thee (your wife's name),
to be my wedded wife;
and I do promise and covenant before God
to be thy loving and faithful husband—

in plenty and want,
in joy and in sorrow,
in sickness and in health,
as long as we both shall live.

P.S. A nice little added touch is to ask your wife for her wedding ring. Then, as you renew your vows, you can slip the ring back on her finger all over again! You can also add these words:

This ring I give thee
In token and pledge,
of our constant faith
and abiding love.

All of the ideas and suggestions in this chapter are meant to help you to express to your wife that you love her. It's all about telling her so...in as many ways as possible. Tell her that you prize her as a friend. Tell her how much you enjoy spending time with her. Tell her you want to go on a date. Tell her you enjoy being in her presence. Tell her of your renewed commitment to show her your love by your life. Tell her that, by God's grace, you intend to faithfully keep those vows one day at a time for the rest of your days, "'til death you do part." Tell her of your love in as many ways as you can think of.

Maybe the poem on the next page will encourage you to "tell her so"...and to tell her now, and to tell her often!

Tell Her So

Amid the cares of married life,
In spite of toil and business strife,
If you value your sweet wife,
Tell her so!

There was a time you thought it bliss
To get the favor of a kiss;
A dozen now won't come amiss–
Tell her so!

Don't act as if she's passed her prime,
As though to please her were a crime–
If e'er you loved her, now's the time;
Tell her so!

You are hers and hers alone;
Well you know she's all your own;
Don't wait to carve it on the stone–
Tell her so!

Never let her heart grow cold;
Richer beauties will unfold.
She is worth her weight in gold;
Tell her so![19]

The Christian family is under attack by the forces of evil. Christian marriages are disintegrating at an alarming rate. Children in Christian homes are not receiving the proper training and modeling from their parents. And, from my perspective, a major contributor to this tragic slide is a husband and father who is not assuming his God-ordained role as spiritual leader.

—Jim George

8
A Heart That Leads Your Wife

Both of them were upright in the sight of God, observing all the Lord's commandments and regulations blamelessly.

—LUKE 1:6

As Elizabeth and I have the opportunity to travel around the country as a part of our speaking ministry, one of the major concerns that women voice to me is that their husbands show little or no desire to be the spiritual leaders in their family. These wives feel awkward because they don't want to step into the role that rightfully belongs to their husbands, and they are fearful of surpassing their husbands in spiritual maturity—to the point where they might leave their husbands so far behind spiritually that their husbands would get discouraged at the idea of even trying to catch up. Therefore, the wives are reluctant to attempt to grow. So when a husband isn't exercising spiritual leadership, it affects the spiritual well-being of the rest of the family.

We Have Met the Enemy...

The cartoon strips in the newspaper are one of my favorite places to find illustrations for my sermons and leadership seminars...and Pogo is one of my favorites. I have one strip in which Pogo is standing on a rock with a George Washington-style paper hat on his head and a small wooden sword in his hand, which he is pointing toward the sky as he declares, "We have met the enemy...and they is us!"

Well, my friend, when it comes to the condition of the Christian family today, we men can often be our own worst enemy. Why would I say this? Because the Christian family is under attack by the forces of evil. Christian marriages are disintegrating at an alarming rate. Children in Christian homes are not receiving the proper training and modeling from their parents. And, from my perspective, a major contributor to this tragic slide is a husband and father who is not assuming his God-ordained role as spiritual leader.

But it's never too late to change that. You and I can begin to turn this slide of the Christian family around. All it takes is a man who is willing to pay the price—one man who is willing to let God take control of his selfish heart, one man who is desiring to become a man after God's own heart, one man who may not make a difference in the world but most definitely can make a difference in his family. And that's what really counts!

My prayer is that you are that man. And that this book will help nurture your desire to become that spiritually maturing leader your wife is longing for. (That continues to be my desire for myself, for I'm still growing in my role as a spiritual leader as well.) Are you up for the challenge? I imagine you are, or you wouldn't have gotten this far in this book.

Like it or not, if you are married, God has placed you, as the husband and father, in charge of your family's spiritual condition. By your own growth—or lack of growth—toward spiritual maturity, you regulate the maturity of your wife and children. That's a scary thought, isn't it? Even more sobering is the fact that God holds you and me—as husbands and fathers—responsible for the spiritual condition of our families.

Now, what exactly does it mean to assume a more active role of leadership in your marriage and family?

Encouraging Your Wife's Spiritual Growth

The most significant way to encourage your wife's spiritual growth is to be growing spiritually yourself. As I said a moment ago, you set the spiritual pace for your wife and for your children.

In some marriages, a wife will wait for her husband to take on the role of spiritual leadership before she takes steps to start growing herself. In other cases, a wife will slow down in her own growth while she waits for her husband to speed up his growth. In both scenarios, the wife is retarded spiritually because of the husband's actions. (Does either of these scenarios describe your wife's frustration?) Friend, this has got to change if you are going to encourage your wife's spiritual growth!

One morning while I was reading my Bible, I came to a passage that really challenged me in my own spiritual growth:

> In the time of Herod king of Judea there was a priest named Zechariah, who belonged to the priestly division of Abijah; his wife Elizabeth was also a descendant of Aaron. *Both of them were upright in the sight of God, observing all the Lord's commandments and regulations blamelessly* (Luke 1:5-6, emphasis added).

These two people—Zechariah and Elizabeth—were about to become the parents of John the Baptist, the herald of the

Messiah, Jesus Christ. God desired a special set of parents for a special child who would have a special mission. As I read this passage, I noticed an immediate application for me: God is asking that *both* my wife and I be growing spiritually. To have the greatest spiritual impact not only in our family but also in ministry, we both need to be growing.

Once you and I as husbands grasp this reality and start growing, we can then begin to assist our wives in their growth. Our assistance may be as simple as having a daily Bible reading schedule that we follow individually and then coming together at the end of the day to compare notes. It may mean we study through a book of the Bible together. Fortunately, there are many study tools that couples can use together. So a lack of resources is no excuse. We as men just need to take the initiative to have a more active role in leading our family spiritually.

Encouraging my wife's spiritual growth doesn't always mean that I have to personally be a part of the growth process. Sometimes I only need to be a "spiritual cheerleader." My role is cheering her on in her growth as she studies the Bible on her own or as she participates in a woman's Bible study. I am still fulfilling my role as the spiritual leader, even though I don't personally teach my wife. I'm there to give her encouragement and direction.

Again, remember your wedding day? You made a vow to nurture your wife. Nurturing her involves both the physical and spiritual areas of life. Therefore you must see that your wife is growing spiritually! And the first step, of course, is asking God to give you a fresh commitment to grow yourself. Then ask your wife how you can best help her grow.

Protecting Your Wife

Let's look again at Ephesians 5 and focus on another element of spiritual leadership in the family—the protective aspect of leadership. In verses 26-27, Paul writes about Christ's commitment to His church—His commitment to...

> ...make her holy, cleansing her by the washing with water through the word, and to present her to himself as a radiant church, without stain or wrinkle or any other blemish, but holy and blameless.

Jesus Christ purposes to present the church to Himself without spot, wrinkle, or blemish. He desires that the church be holy and spotless. And to do this, He constantly protects her. He watches out for her purity. This, then, is God's picture to you and me, as men after His own heart, of what it means to be the loving spiritual protector. We are to protect our wives from the influences and onslaughts of the world.

How are you doing in protecting your wife? Or are you out there doing your own thing, oblivious to what's going on at home or in her life?

It appears that's what Adam was doing in the Garden of Eden (Genesis 3:1-5) when Eve was approached by the serpent. Where was Adam when Satan began to question Eve about God's wisdom and God's love for her and Adam? And why didn't Adam step in and defend both his wife and God's character? The Bible doesn't answer any of these questions, but maybe...just maybe...if Adam had been there, things would have turned out a whole lot differently!

Now, think back again to those vows you stated at your wedding. Somewhere in the ceremony the minister probably mentioned something from Ephesians 5 about protecting your wife from the world. That's a major responsibility for you as a husband! And here are some practical suggestions on how you can do that (which I learned the hard way, of course!):

- Pray for your wife's purity and protection daily. You can do this during your quiet time each morning. Or, you can pray for her while you're driving to work (or while you're running, etc.).
- Determine together if the place where your wife works is a healthy environment for her spiritually. (Ask this question of any potential job as well.)
- Be aware of what she's watching on TV. (Remember Adam—maybe he should have been more involved in his wife's life!)
- Shield her from people who might have a negative effect on her spiritual growth. (Such a person could be anyone who has a destructive influence on her, even a relative or a friend.)

You might be looking at this checklist and thinking, *This list is for my teenage daughter, not my wife!* Yes, these principles could be applicable to your daughter as well. You are right—and wise—to be concerned for your daughter's purity. So you lovingly, protectively watch what she does, where she goes, and who she goes out with.

But this checklist also says, "I love my wife and I lovingly protect her purity, too!" Just because your wife is an adult doesn't release you from your responsibility to protect her spiritual purity and emotional well-being. What wife wouldn't appreciate a husband who shows this kind of love and concern?

Ways to Love by Leading

By now you may be feeling a bit overwhelmed by what it means to love by leading. You may have thought that by providing for your wife financially, you are demonstrating your love. (I did!) You have probably thought that through physical intimacy, you are demonstrating your love. (I did!) These are legitimate expressions of love, but true love, biblical love, Christlike love, goes way beyond the physical to the spiritual and emotional.

To begin loving by leading, the first thing to remember is that it's never too late to get started! I remember running in a relay race while in high school. After the first leg of the race, our team seemed hopelessly behind. We could have given up and dropped out. But we didn't. Each man gave a little extra effort…and we ended up placing in the race. That's all God is asking of you—that you give leadership in your marriage your best shot. Don't give up. Don't *ever* give up! Instead, get into the race for God and your wife. Both God and your wife deserve your best effort.

Let me now give you a few further suggestions on loving by leading:

Start growing yourself—I know I'm repeating myself with this point, but it's important! The most significant way to love your wife is to be growing yourself. Is your wife waiting and praying for God to light a fire under you so you would desire to grow? Here are a few easy steps any man can take to get started:

- Follow a schedule for reading your Bible daily (like the one on pages 251-63). Remember, the Bible is supernatural, and it will do supernatural things in your life and in your marriage. But you must start the process by reading it.
- Find someone to disciple you. "As iron sharpens iron, so one man sharpens another" (Proverbs 27:17).
- Avoid people who drag you down spiritually. "Do not be misled: 'Bad company corrupts good character'" (1 Corinthians 15:33).

- Avoid tempting situations. "Flee the evil desires of youth" (2 Timothy 2:22).
- Don't flirt with compromising situations. "Do not think about how to gratify the desires of the sinful nature" (Romans 13:14).

Start giving spiritual guidance—Encourage your wife to get involved in a women's Bible study at the church. Then with genuine interest ask questions each week about the study and what she is learning. You don't need to teach her the Bible yourself to be the spiritual leader. Just make sure she is pointed in the right direction and take joy in her progress.

Start praying together—A number of years ago a couple came to me with a marriage problem. We worked through the issues, and then I asked the husband to pray and to commit our discussion to the Lord. When he had finished praying, I looked up to find the wife crying. She said, "We have been married ten years, and this is the first time we have prayed together as a couple." Don't let that be your wife's tearful confession. Friend, start taking leadership and pray with and for your wife.

Start leading with understanding—The Bible refers to your wife as "the weaker partner": "Husbands...be considerate as you live with your wives, and treat them with respect as the weaker partner and as heirs with you of the gracious gift of life, so that nothing will hinder your prayers" (1 Peter 3:7). One resource clarifies the word "weaker" in this way: "While she is fully equal in Christ and not inferior spiritually because she is a woman (see Galatians 3:28), she is physically weaker, and in need of protection, provision, and strength from her husband."[20]

The fact that your wife is weaker physically is not meant to reflect on her negatively. It's simply an affirmation of her need for protection and provision. In your marriage, you need to assume a leadership role so that you can literally "shoulder" more of the physical responsibilities in your lives and your home.

You may think that if you bring home the paycheck, you have fulfilled your leadership obligations in the home. (That's how I thought!) After all, you're "providing"! Oh, you may do a few chores around the house if harassed long enough, but otherwise you, like most men, are content to let your wife shoulder most of the responsibilities for the care of the house (inside and out), the cars, the bills, the children, any and all salesmen who come to the door, and both sets of parents—all while holding down a full-time job!

Let's do the math. Let's say you work eight or nine hours a day and drive a one-hour commute, perhaps five or six days a week. Does your wife also work eight or nine hours a day? And does she then come home to be a wife, mother, chef, nurse, homemaker, gardener, handyman, referee, and administrator? If so, this works out to be at *least* a second full-time job! Some people would call this a "twenty-four/seven." Now I ask you, does that seem to be a little out of balance?

Could your wife's physical load use lightening? Here are some ways to help:

- Sit down with your wife and go over her schedule. Are there areas where better time management might help relieve some pressure?

- Take a greater responsibility for household duties (especially if you both work). Remember, you are a team. The house and all that's inside and out belongs to both of you. Why shouldn't you both assume some of the responsibilities?

- Assume the burden of hassling salesmen, plumbers, car mechanics, and any other situation where your wife would have to confront a man over issues having to do with family affairs.

- Share in the financial decisions. Some men handle all the finances in the home, and the wife does nothing and knows nothing. Other men allow their wife to handle the finances, and they in turn know nothing and do nothing. Now, somewhere between these two opposites is a balance. I think we would both agree that the main burden of earning money and practicing wise financial stewardship should ultimately fall on the shoulders of the husband (1 Timothy 5:8). But all aspects of marriage are a shared responsibility, including the finances. Together, you and your wife should decide who does what in the financial area and make sure the other is informed and involved in the process.

- Take a more active role in your children's lives. Help your wife with the physical, mental, and spiritual nurturing of the children. As the spiritual leader of the family, read Bible stories to your children every night as part of the bedtime routine. Also, assist your children with memorizing some key Bible verses about Jesus Christ and the Christian faith.

- Honor your wife. Do you want to have an open line of communication with God? Then treat your wife with respect and honor (1 Peter 3:7). There is no other person on the face of this earth whom you should honor more than your wife.

Wow! There is so much that God wants to do with and through you and your mate as a couple! But this need not feel overwhelming—not at all. It all comes down to one very simple principle:

> "Husbands, love your wives" (Ephesians 5:25).

Loving your wife is the starting point of becoming a husband who cherishes, protects, and nourishes. No husband wakes up in the morning and says, "I think I won't love my wife today." Yet by our actions or lack of actions, we may be doing just that. We may inadvertently choose not to love our wives by not doing something for or with them. Don't let this be you. Start following God's command to love your wife so that this can be said of the two of you:

> Both of them were upright in the sight of God, observing all the Lord's commandments and regulations blamelessly (Luke 1:6).

As your *heart goes, so goes your* family! *If your* heart *isn't right, no childraising system, rules, or gimmicks will ever work. As your* heart *goes, so goes your* parenting!

—JIM GEORGE

9
A Heart That Loves Your Children

Fathers, do not exasperate your children; instead, bring them up in the training and instruction of the Lord.

—EPHESIANS 6:4

While writing this chapter, I found in my notes a copy of an article from *Newsweek* magazine entitled "Dear Dads: Save Your Sons." The writer, Mr. Christopher N. Bacorn, a trained psychologist in Texas, lamented the fact that most of the youthful offenders of gang violence, guns, and drugs were males. In the article he asked the question, "Where are the fathers?" He then answered, "Well, I can tell you where they're not. They're not at PTA meetings or piano recitals. They're not teaching Sunday school. You won't find them in the pediatrician's office, holding a sick child...."

Mr. Bacorn then posed this question,

> What would happen if the truant fathers of America began spending time with their children?...If these fathers were to spend more

> time with their children, it just might have an effect on the future of marriage and divorce. Not only do many boys lack a sense of how a man should behave; many girls don't know either, having little exposure themselves to healthy male-female relationships.[21]

The psychologist ended the article with what he called "a measure of hopelessness" as he concluded that the American father is nowhere to be found.

You know, without Jesus Christ in our lives, we too might be an "absentee father." We too might be on the golf course, tennis court, bowling alley, on the lake fishing, or working from early morning to late at night. We too might be watching the national average of six-plus hours of television per day. In short, without a biblical understanding of our God-given priorities as a man after God's own heart, we would be everywhere...except in the company of our children.

Living Out Your Beliefs

Fortunately for us as Christian husbands and fathers, God has given us specific directions in the Bible for our roles and responsibilities. In Ephesians 5 we received our marching orders for our relationships with our wives. And then Ephesians 6 gives us these guidelines for parenting our children:

> Fathers, do not exasperate your children; instead, bring them up in the training and instruction of the Lord (Ephesians 6:4).

As a point of reference, the apostle Paul wrote the book of Ephesians to a group of Christians in Ephesus, a city in Asia Minor. It was a large city that provided lots of opportunities to sin. (This sounds like where I live!) God used Paul to plant a church in this very pagan city, and Paul faithfully taught this fledgling church for three years. Several years later, Paul wrote to these people to further assist them with their struggles against the world around them and its influence on their marriage and family relationships.

How did Paul do this? In the first half of Ephesians he laid down a doctrinal foundation for his readers, giving them important truths they could believe and stand on. Then in the second half of the book he explained how to live out these truths, beginning with these words: "live a life worthy of the calling you have received" (Ephesians 4:1). In essence, Paul is saying, "Take the truths I have given you about your relationship with God, beloved brothers and sisters in Christ, and live out your beliefs in your relationships at home." Paul is saying that one's behavior always reflects belief.

Parenting Is a Partnership

Friend, Paul's call to live out what you believe speaks to you and me today. What we believe and obey of God's Word will affect how we live our lives. And this applies to loving our wives and caring for our children.

Let me backtrack for a minute to your relationship with your wife. God says to us husbands, "Husbands, love your wives" (Ephesians 5:25). How we love and care for our wives is a major factor in caring for our children. Why? Because parenting is a partnership. Let me explain…

As you love and care for your wife, she will have a sense of well-being. This, in turn, enables her to better focus her attention on the children. Because of the significant and unique role a mother plays in the lives of her children, your wife's sense of well-being will affect how she influences and cares for your children. So through loving your wife, you are having an impact on your children. That's one way that parenting is a partnership.

This doesn't mean you can abdicate your duties as a father. God still requires something of you. He requires that you as a father bring your children up "in the training and instruction of the Lord." And when you love your wife, she will eagerly shoulder that responsibility with you. By working as partners, you'll find the task of parenting much easier. So, as you continue to read about your responsibilities in caring for your children, always keep in mind that one key to your success as a father (on the human level) is your love for your wife. You might want to take a moment now to offer up a prayer of thanksgiving for the *mother* of your children—your wife! She is a special lady, and she deserves not only your prayers, but also your verbal and physical affirmation. Take Solomon's advice—"may you ever be captivated by her love" (Proverbs 5:19).

Dealing with the Heart

This book is about the heart and its affection for God and the priorities He sets for our lives as men. So as we begin to talk about our children, we must begin with a "heart exam."

Your Heart

The heart is the place where our life gets its direction. It's been called the "control center of life."[22] And because God created us, He knows us and our hearts. This is Jesus' estimation of the significance of the heart and its connection to our conduct:

> The good man brings good things out of the good stored up in his heart, and the evil man brings evil things out of the evil stored up in his

> heart. For out of the overflow of his heart his mouth speaks (Luke 6:45).

As we discussed earlier from King David's example, a man after God's own heart is a man who has a God-ward heart. His heart has its affections set first and foremost on God. Jesus said we are to

> "Love the LORD your God with all your heart and with all your soul and with all your mind." This is the first and greatest commandment. And the second is like it: "Love your neighbor as yourself" (Matthew 22:37-39).

Your love for God will naturally affect your relationships with those around you. It works like this: If you love the Lord your God, you will love your neighbor. And who are your closest neighbors? Your wife and children! Just as your wife receives the blessings of your relationship with God, so your children will also receive those same blessings.

Consider what one of my former students, Dennis Wilson, says in his book on parenting about the impact a father's relationship with God has on his family:

> The order of priorities is evident: One must be seeking the Lord with his own heart before instructing his children in God's ways. Although we will never live out our roles as fathers perfectly, our genuine desire and efforts to continually love, obey, and grow in our knowledge of God can be felt by the entire family.[23]

So again, take a heart exam—as *your* heart goes, so goes your *family!* If your *heart* isn't right, no childraising system, rules, or gimmicks will ever work. As your *heart* goes, so goes your *parenting!*

Your Children's Hearts

Just as your relationship with God affects your conduct, so your children's conduct will be determined by their heart-relationship with God. Therefore, we must be concerned for our children's hearts. This is the starting point for caring for our children. Author Tedd Tripp says it well:

> ...parenting is concerned with shepherding the heart. You must learn to work back from the behavior you see to the heart, exposing heart issues for your children. In short, you must learn to engage them, not just reprove them. Help them see the ways that they are trying to slake [satisfy] their soul's thirst with that which cannot satisfy. You must help your kids gain a clear focus on the cross of Christ.

Here is the proposition: Behavior is heart driven. Therefore, correction, discipline and training—all parenting—must be addressed to the heart. The fundamental task of parenting is shepherding the hearts of your children.[24]

Did you catch that closing statement? The fundamental task of parenting is shepherding the hearts of our children. Your children are given to you by God, and their hearts are your stewardship from God. And He expects you to do your part in raising them to know and love Him.

Passing On a Love for God

Let's learn a parenting lesson now from the Old Testament. After the Israelites were freed from their bondage in Egypt, and just before they entered the Promised Land, God gave them instructions about focusing their whole heart on Him and then passing that affection on to their children:

> Love the LORD your God with all your heart and with all your soul and with all your strength. These commandments that I give you today are to be upon *your* hearts. Impress them on *your* children. Talk about them when you sit at home and when you walk along the road, when you lie down and when you get up (Deuteronomy 6:5-7, emphases added).

Did you notice the extent of the parents' responsibilities? First they were responsible to have an intimate relationship with God. Then they were responsible to pass on their love for God to their children. The parents were to diligently teach their children to love God at any and every opportunity. In the home, out of the home, on the road...at all times. And friend, God is asking the same of you and me as dads today. We are to love God, and we are to pass on that same love for God to our children.

It's been said that the mind is a terrible thing to neglect. But far more tragic is a soul that has been left to neglect. I had this fact brought home to me in a sad way recently. I was asking a mother where she went to church. She said that she had just started going back to church again. Then with great remorse in her voice, she related how her daughter had wanted to go to church when she was younger, but now as a teenager she doesn't have that desire anymore. When the daughter had begged to go to church, the parent wasn't interested. And now it was too late!

The Puritans had a sobering perspective on raising children and the eternal consequence of our actions:

> It's in your hand to do them the greatest kindness or cruelty in all the world: help them to know God and to be saved, and you do more for them than if you helped them to be Lords or princes: if you neglect their souls, and breed them in ignorance, worldliness, ungodliness, and sin, you betray them to the devil, the enemy of souls, even as truly as if you sold them to him; you seal them to be slaves to Satan; you betray them to him that will deceive them and abuse them in this life, and torment them in the next.[25]

If that's not enough to motivate you to assume a greater role in the spiritual training of your children, hear what Jesus had to say about the spiritual care of your children:

> If anyone causes one of these little ones who believe in me to sin, it would be better for him to have a large millstone hung around his neck and to be drowned in the depths of the sea. Woe to the world because of the things that cause people [children] to sin! Such things must come, but woe to the man through whom they come! (Matthew 18:6-7).

Ways to Influence Your Children

Congratulations—you've made it this far! I know this chapter has been a little heavy. But when you think about it, we're talking about shaping the entire future of a child's life, and influencing his or her eternal destiny. I hope you've felt the gravity of your obligation to God…and to your children. Here are some steps for getting started. They're simple, but they will require a lot from you. However, the rewards of being a godly husband and father are well worth it!

Start by loving your wife—God designed parents to be partners, and a key essential to caring for your children is showing a godly love for your wife.

Start by taking your family to church—Perhaps your spiritual life isn't going in the right direction at this time. But the simple act of getting your family to church is a giant step toward assuming the spiritual leadership of your family.

Start by growing spiritually—The answer to all that we've talked about in past chapters and all that we will talk about in the upcoming chapters is summed up in spiritual maturity. A man after God's own heart is a man who constantly desires to grow spiritually. He's never where he wants to be, but he's always striving to be where he needs to be.

Start by spending time with your children—This one's obvious. A closer relationship with your children comes only with time.

Start by modeling Christlike behavior—As you start to mature in your walk with Christ, you will assume more of a leadership posture in your family. You can then say to your children, "Follow my example, as I follow the example of Christ" (1 Corinthians 11:1). There is no greater force for spiritual change (on the human level) than that of a godly father's example before the watching eyes of young, moldable hearts!

Friend, there's no need for this priority from God to be overwhelming. Love your wife. Take your family to church. Grow spiritually. Spend time with the family. Live out your Christianity. It's in your hands as a father to care for your children. You already make great sacrifices every day for their physical well-being. For example, you plan and save for their education, you make sure they get to their sporting events, you make all sorts of sacrifices for the earthly things in life. Now let's commit ourselves afresh to make just as great—or greater!—sacrifices to point our children toward God. Let's do all we can. Don't procrastinate! There is a celestial struggle going on for the soul of your precious child. Do your part and point them toward God.

Ten Commandments for Childraising

I. Teach them, using God's Word.
(Deuteronomy 6:4-9)

II. Tell them what's right and wrong.
(1 Kings 1:6)

III. See them as gifts from God.
(Psalm 127:3)

IV. Guide them in godly ways.
(Proverbs 22:6)

V. Discipline them.
(Proverbs 29:17)

VI. Love them unconditionally.
(Luke 15:11-32)

VII. Do not provoke them to wrath.
(Ephesians 6:4)

VIII. Earn their respect by example.
(1 Timothy 3:4)

IX. Provide for their physical needs.
(1 Timothy 5:8)

X. Pass your faith along to them.
(2 Timothy 1:5)[26]

Providing a spiritual covering by bringing our children before God's throne through prayer is one of the unique privileges that you and I have as fathers. You may not comprehend what a rare opportunity you have until you realize that, with the exception of your wife's prayers and possibly a faithful believing grandparent's prayers, you may be the only other person on the face of this earth who is praying for your children. Don't miss out on this blessed privilege!

—JIM GEORGE

10
A Heart That Leads Your Children

These commandments that I give you today are to be upon your hearts. Impress them on your children.

—DEUTERONOMY 6:6-7

At the beginning of this book I shared with you my testimony as the "prodigal son" who came home to his father (Luke 15:11-31). As a young boy I went to church, but when I left for college, the things of God were of little interest to me. Not until age 30 did I recognize that I was spiritually malnourished...and horribly so!

What I haven't mentioned yet is what faced me when I returned "home" spiritually. I had a new believing wife and two small children, two-and-a-half years old and one-and-a-half. I was now to be the spiritual head of my family and I didn't have a clue as to where to start. I thank God that I at least realized I needed to get my family to a good Bible-teaching church where we all began to be fed and get direction for our lives.

Anyway, once I arrived at the church, I started looking and praying for someone who could give me some help, some guidance, anything that would assist me in being a godly husband and a loving, caring father to my girls. And the Lord answered my prayers. I found a church elder who was able to give me some biblical direction. John gave me some valuable principles from God's Word and from his own life experiences, and these were a constant source of input for the next 25 years of my own life as a parent. I'm so glad that several years ago I went to his house and thanked John and his wife personally for the advice and example they were to me and Elizabeth. What a blessing they have been to our family! My prayer for you is that this book—and perhaps a spiritually mature man at your church—will aid you in fulfilling your role of providing leadership for your family.

In the previous chapter, we looked at what it means to be a godly father. You may be where I was when I started—minus ten on a scale of one to ten! But that's OK. Once you take those first steps toward growth by loving your wife, going to church, spending time with the kids, and beginning to model Christlike behavior, you will see some changes occur, both in your family and in you. Now, let's go just a bit further with a few more steps.

Your Provision for Your Children

Provide an Active Role in Teaching

When you take the time to provide spiritual guidance for your children, you fulfill a significant role in the spiritual development of your family. Just as a pastor leads his flock, you as a father can lead your "little flock" toward a better understanding of God through the study of His Word, family prayers, and even singing praises. Read J. I. Packer's description of how the Puritans of old encouraged the fathers, as the priests of their families, to lead and instruct their household:

> It was the husband's responsibility to channel the family into religion; to take them to church on the Lord's Day, and oversee the sanctifying of that entire day in the home; to catechize the children, and teach them the faith; to examine the whole family after each sermon, to see how much had been retained and understood, and to fill any gaps in understanding that might remain; to lead the family in worship daily, ideally twice a day; and to set an example of sober godliness at all times and in all matters.[27]

As you can see, the Puritans saw the role of teacher as an important function of the father's duties. Maybe you're not quite ready to take on all the spiritual duties of the Puritan father (and I admit, it's quite a list!), but you can begin where you are. Again, if you don't know where to start, ask a godly man at church for help. Look for a man who clearly has his act together with respect to his family. Ask for advice or discipleship in this matter of teaching your children; don't be too proud to ask for help. The stakes are too high. There is a spiritual battle going on for the hearts and minds of your children. As Tedd Tripp writes, "Parents are engaged in hand-to-hand combat on the world's smallest battlefield, their children's hearts."[28]

Christian dad, you *must* take the leadership in this important task! Don't delegate this responsibility to your wife. Together, the two of you should determine the best way to carry out this essential activity of shepherding your children's hearts. And don't leave it to the Sunday school teacher at church, to the youth pastor, or to a fine Christian school. It's *your* responsibility. And fulfilling this responsibility, with God's enablement, is what a man after God's own heart does...and does heartily (even if it's scary at first!).

Are you thinking you're too busy? Busyness is not an excuse for neglecting the teaching of your children. Most families are extremely busy, and yours is no exception. If something is important, somehow you find the time to do it, don't you? Especially when you consider that we are talking about your children's eternal destiny.

So, when do we dads do this essential task? Where do we fit "the family altar" into an already busy schedule? For most of us, it has to be one of two predictable times—either in the morning at the breakfast table before going to work, or in the evening at dinner. Finding the time will always be the harder task. Determining what content to teach will be much easier. Again, ask your pastor or someone who has been successful at family devotions what you can share with your family. Don't betray your children to the devil because of your neglect. Instead, take an active role in teaching your children to follow God.

Provide a Consistent Godly Example

I've served in a lot of ministries in my former churches. At one point, I was the pastor of evangelism. While in that capacity I visited with the leaders of several of the major outreach ministries on the University of California Los Angeles (UCLA) campus. I asked these men to tell me who, in their opinion, were the most difficult students to reach for Jesus Christ. Without exception and without hesitation, they all reported it was the children of nominal Christian parents. It seems the students from such homes wanted nothing to do with a religion that hadn't been lived out in their family.

Friend, the greatest influence you can have on your children will come from your Christian example at home. The reality of Christ is nowhere better demonstrated than in your consistent, godly conduct at home. I know I've mentioned these principles from Deuteronomy 6:6-7 before, but they're worth repeating. Moses instructed parents to diligently teach God's Word to their children...

when you sit at home,
when you walk along the road,
when you lie down,
when you get up.

The father who does this is assuming an active role as a teacher and is dedicated to providing a consistent godly example. And *this* is the kind of father you want to become!

It's clear that an inconsistent example can have a negative effect, and that a consistent godly example will bear eternal rewards. Take, for example, Timothy, who was discipled by the apostle Paul. Paul reminds Timothy of the godly examples he had at home (2 Timothy 1:5), and later in the same letter he states the impact of that example...which led to a knowledge of "the holy Scriptures, which are able to make you wise for salvation through faith in Christ Jesus" (2 Timothy 3:15). As you take the time to care for your own spiritual growth, you will most definitely show your children the reality of Christ in your life. Your consistent example as a godly father will have the greatest human influence on your children's spiritual direction.

Provide Constant Leadership

Being the spiritual leader of your family is a *constant* role that never changes as long as you have a family. Though it may be a challenge to find the time to provide that leadership consistently, the benefits make it well worthwhile. But what about those times when you're away from home? If you're like me, your job may take you out of town for extended periods of time. During such times, you can delegate your leadership to your wife. In my case, I was away for a two-week period of time each year as an Army reservist. At other times I would be away on missions trips. Each time, before I left home, I talked with Elizabeth and verbally handed over my responsibilities for her to assume in my absence. And one of those responsibilities—the main one—was carrying on our daughters' spiritual instruction.

You, too, as God's leader, may need to delegate the responsibility of continuing the normal spiritual training activities with the children to your wife in your absence. Then when you return, be prepared to quickly reassume your role. At times you and your wife may have to flex with changes—but as soon as possible, you must return to your leadership role. This role is such a high priority that no job, hobby, or anything else should permanently interfere with this constant duty for you as a man after God's own heart.

Are you struggling with your role as the spiritual leader in your family? That's OK! This shows you are realizing the importance of your role and just aren't quite sure how to pull it off. I was in the same place many years ago, so I can identify. Pray that God would provide a godly example for you in your church. Sit regularly under the teaching of that man and let him teach you the Bible's principles for spiritual leadership and biblical parenting. These are God's principles, so they work. Trust in them over the long haul and apply them faithfully throughout the childrearing years. And just as I am now sharing with you about some of my training, you can one day give other younger men the benefit of your training and life experiences in biblical parenting.

Provide Consistent Discipline

The Bible has much to say about disciplining our children. In fact, the Bible teaches us that God's discipline in our lives is a sign that we are His beloved sons:

> The LORD disciplines those he loves, as a father the son he delights in (Proverbs 3:12).
>
> The Lord disciplines those he loves, and he punishes everyone he accepts as a son....For what son is not disciplined by his father (Hebrews 12:6-7)?

Because God is perfectly just and wise, His discipline of you and me as sons is consistently and fairly administered. And the discipline we administer to our children should be carried out in the same way. Evidently this wasn't the case of some fathers in the New Testament. Consider the caution that Paul gives to two kinds of fathers concerning the treatment of their children:

1. "Fathers, do not *embitter* your children, or they will become discouraged" (Colossians 3:21, emphasis added).

The word "embitter" means to excite, to provoke, to irritate. And to "become discouraged" means to lose heart, to be without courage or spirit, to become spiritless, to go about a task in a listless, moody, sullen way. A child who is frequently irritated by over-severity or injustice generally acquires a spirit of sullen resignation, leading to despair.

Sometimes in our zeal to be the leader and the disciplinarian, we can end up reacting to the actions of our children in an inconsistent and harsh manner. Then, over a period of time, as we continually crush their spirits, the children withdraw...until one day, when they are old enough, they walk away. We will have fulfilled our duty, but with disastrous results.

2. "Fathers, do not *exasperate* your children" (Ephesians 6:4, emphasis added).

Again, Paul is warning fathers how *not* to treat their children. The word "exasperate" means to anger, to make angry, to bring one along to a deep-seated anger. In his book *Successful Christian Parenting*, Dr. John MacArthur comments on this verse:

> This is a caution, a warning, designed to put parents on guard against stirring their children's anger either deliberately or through careless but unnecessary provocations. There are times, of course, when children become sinfully angry with their parents apart from any provocation....But there are other times when the parents are guilty of provoking their children's anger by thoughtlessly aggravating them, by deliberately goading them, by callously neglecting them, or by any number of other intentional or careless means that exasperate them. When that happens, it is the parents who are sinning—and provoking the child to sin as well.[29]

Yes, the Bible speaks of using discipline— "He who spares the rod hates his son, but he who loves him is careful to discipline him" (Proverbs 13:24). But it also warns us to discipline in love, using appropriate and consistent methods.

Even though your children may not immediately appreciate the discipline, if you administer it consistently and fairly, they will ultimately see it as such. They will see the discipline as coming from a loving father who cares about his children.

Finally, it's very important that you and your wife agree on *how*, *when*, *where* you correct your children, and *why*. The two of you need to determine beforehand how you are going to deal with the different types of wrong behavior in your children. I'm sure you have already learned that no two children are alike! Each child will need to be disciplined differently, but you will also need to maintain consistency with all the children. Remember—the best way to negate the usefulness of discipline is to be inconsistent!

Provide Intercessory Prayers for Your Children

Praying for your children is another aspect of being the spiritual head of your family. You want to pray for God's saving grace in their lives, for their spiritual growth, for God's continued working in their lives, and for their future mates. (I prayed faithfully for godly husbands for my girls for over 20 years, and I am humbled every day as I praise God that He answered my prayers with two godly sons-in-law.)

Whenever I think of a father who prays for his children, I immediately think of Job in the Old Testament and his ministry on behalf of his children:

> His sons used to take turns holding feasts in their homes, and they would invite their three sisters to eat and drink with them. When a period of feasting had run its course, Job would send and have them purified. Early in the morning he would sacrifice a burnt offering for each of them, thinking, "Perhaps my children have sinned and curse God in their hearts." This was Job's regular custom (Job 1:4-5).

Bringing our children before God's throne through prayer is one of the unique privileges that you and I have as fathers. You may not comprehend what a rare opportunity you have until you realize that, with the exception of your wife's prayers and possibly the prayers of believing grandparents, you may be the only other person on the face of this earth who is praying for your children. Don't miss out on this privilege!

Provide a Godly Influence Outside the Home

There's no doubt the home is the focal point for shepherding your children. The home is the training ground for godly living. But there are times when your children are away from home, and away from your influence. What can you do? You'll want to do whatever you can to make sure your children are influenced by other godly people outside your home.

The church is the second most influential place where your children can receive godly influences. At church, your children can be influenced by Sunday school teachers, youth leaders, and dedicated pastors. (Our girls had some wonderful teachers and youth leaders over the years.)

To make this happen, you need to be excited about church yourself, and make sure your children get to church. Even though they may balk at times, don't give in. As the shepherd of your little flock, make sure your children are being fed from God's Word, at church, under the influence of godly teachers and youth leaders.

Provide Discernment for Outside Influences

Outside of your home and church, there will be times when your children will be influenced by people who are somewhat beyond your control. Your children will encounter situations and influences that are not godly. This may happen at a public school, or with neighborhood children, or with others out in the world. You, as the spiritual head, must provide discernment as much as possible. Who are their friends at school? Where are they spending their time? What are they reading and viewing?

You must also be training the spiritual sensitivity of your children so that they can "distinguish good from evil" (Hebrews 5:14). Your children will grow up, go off to school, and start dating. All of these activities are natural and normal. You're not always going to be there for your children. They will be in situations that require them to make some life decisions on their own. And before that happens, you want to give them spiritual discernment. You want them to learn how to make godly choices on their own. That's the ultimate goal of a godly father.

Your Priorities for Your Children

Are you beginning to understand God's priorities for you and your family? A man after God's own heart loves God and desires to be obedient to the Word of God. This means he loves his wife and that together they actively partner in the care of their children. God's man is also thankful to his God for providing a loving, caring mother for his children. He recognizes that her support is vital and essential. But his care and concern for the children is just as vital. He understands that "sons are a heritage from the LORD, children a reward from him" (Psalm 127:3). Therefore, he takes seriously God's admonition to "bring them up in the training and instruction of the Lord" (Ephesians 6:4).

Friend, you have a choice to either "bring up" or "bring down" your children. I know that with the Lord's help, you will continue to make the right choices for each one of them.

—To Bring Down a Son—

1. Let him have plenty of spending money.
2. Permit him to choose his own companions without restraint or direction.
3. Give him a latch-key and allow him to return home late at night.
4. Make no inquiry as to where and with whom he spends his leisure moments.
5. Give him to understand that manners make a good substitute for morals.
6. Teach him to expect pay for every act of helpfulness to others.
7. Be careful never to let him hear your voice in prayer for his salvation and spiritual growth.

—To Bring Up a Son—

1. Make home the brightest and most attractive place on earth.
2. Make him responsible for the performance of a limited number of daily duties.
3. Never punish him in anger.
4. Do not ridicule his conceits (vanity), but rather talk frankly on matters in which he is interested.
5. Let him feel free to invite his friends to your home and table.
6. Be careful to impress upon his mind that making character is more important than making money.

7. Live Christ before him all the time, then you will be able to talk Christ to him with power.
8. Be much in prayer for his salvation and spiritual growth.[30]

The answer isn't for you to ditch your workplace and join a monastery. It's to stay where you are and begin to capture your workplace—any workplace—for Christ. Imagine getting up in the morning not dreading but dedicated to going to work for a purpose—His purpose for you in your workplace! You may never change the entire corporate culture where you work, but you can change lives—your own and many others as well.[31]

—JOHN TRENT, PH.D.

11
A Heart That Is Diligent at Work

So whether you eat or drink or whatever you do,
do it all for the glory of God.

—1 Corinthians 10:31

Rumor has it that work is a consequence of the Fall of man—that if Adam hadn't eaten that apple, we wouldn't have to work today. But in reality, work existed before the Fall. Long before Adam ate that apple, we witness God at work in the creation of the universe.

In Genesis 1:1 we meet God punching the time clock, so to speak, as a worker: "In the beginning God created the heavens and the earth." There was a lot of work to be done, for "the earth was formless and empty" (verse 2). From this point all the way through Genesis 2:1, we have a "work log," if you please, describing God's work of creation. Finally, when the work was complete, God "rested from all the *work* of creating that he had done" (Genesis 2:3, emphasis added).

God modeled for all, and forever, the inherent dignity of work. Then, after He created the universe, He did one final creative act—He "created man in His own image" (Genesis 1:27), and instructed man to...

- fill the earth and subdue it (1:28),
- rule over every living creature (1:28),
- work and take care of the Garden of Eden (2:15), and
- name all the animals (2:19-20).

From this creation account we can see that when God created man in His own image, man, like God Himself, was to be a worker. All of God's work of creation and man's work in the Garden took place before the Fall and the curse!

So the belief that work is a consequence of the Fall is not true. But what *is* true is that as a result of the Fall and the introduction of sin into the world, our work is more difficult! As God said to Adam, "by the sweat of your brow you will eat your food" (Genesis 3:19).

Work Is the Norm

Throughout the Bible, work is seen as a normal and natural part of a man's life. The Old Testament book of Proverbs often contrasts work and those who labor with those who don't or won't work and the consequences of their lack of diligence. For instance:

> He who works his land will have abundant food, but he who chases fantasies lacks judgment (12:11).
>
> All hard work brings a profit, but mere talk leads only to poverty (14:23).
>
> Do you see a man skilled in his work? He will serve before kings; he will not serve before obscure men (22:29).

In the New Testament, the apostle Paul teaches with his life what it means to be a hardworking, bi-vocational missionary:

Paul's example—Listen as Paul defends himself against accusations that he was using the ministry for personal gains.

> You yourselves know how you ought to follow our example. We were not idle when we were with you, nor did we eat anyone's food without paying for it. On the contrary, we worked night and day, laboring and toiling so that we would not be a burden to any of you (2 Thessalonians 3:7-8).

Paul's exhortation—Having modeled what it means to be a hard worker, Paul next reminded the men in the church of this standard:

> When we were with you, we gave you this rule: "If a man will not work, he shall not eat" (2 Thessalonians 3:10).

Paul's encouragement—Paul then encouraged all the men to get busy and go about the business of working:

> We hear that some among you are idle. They are not busy; they are busybodies. Such people we command and urge in the Lord Jesus Christ to settle down and earn the bread they eat (2 Thessalonians 3:11-12).

Paul worked. And he worked hard, and he worked long hours. And he expected every other man to work hard, too! It's the norm. As you take a minute to think about your work habits, how do they measure up?

Work Is Beneficial

Friend, it's obvious God created us to be workers. He knows that our physical and mental makeup thrives on work. Therefore He commands that we work and provide for our families. This, then, becomes another of the priorities we've been talking about. A man after God's own heart loves and obeys God, loves and leads his wife, loves and cares for his children, and he works and provides for his family.

This priority of work is affirmed in the Bible in verse after verse. God knows what is best for us as men. And, would you be surprised to find out that our obedience in relation to work is also beneficial to our health?

That's right. It's been medically proven that physical and mental work helps us to stay healthy and productive! Back in 400 B.C., Hippocrates, the father of medicine, stated, "All parts of the body which are designed for a definite use are kept in health and in enjoyment of fair growth and of long youth by the fulfillment of that use, by their suitable exercise in the duty for which they were made."[32] And in our day, Dr. Charles Mayo of the famed Mayo Clinic builds upon Hippocrates' findings that "worry...profoundly affects the health." But, Mayo adds, "I have never known a man who died from overwork."[33]

Work is most definitely beneficial. That is affirmed by insurance statistics, which reveal that a high percentage of men die within the first year after their retirement.

Work as a Calling

What do you picture when you hear the word *calling?* Most of us immediately think of some form of vocational ministry. We often hear a pastor or missionary say, "I was called into the ministry." The apostle Paul spoke of himself as "called" to be an apostle of Jesus Christ (1 Corinthians 1:1). But what if I were to tell you that your vocation—the job you have right now—is a calling as well?

Webster defines the word *vocation* as coming to us from the Latin *vocatio,* which means "a calling." And the English word means "a call or summons"; specifically, "a calling to a particular state, business, or profession." Just as a pastor or missionary passionately serves God because of the "calling" on his life, so we too should be passionately serving God in our work, or our calling.

In my life I have had many "callings." One of those included being called into the ministry. In fact, I have even written a chapter in a book on pastoral ministries about the call to the ministry.[34] But, like the apostle Paul, who was a missionary *and* a tentmaker, I have provided for my family as a pharmacist, an Army reservist, a pharmaceutical salesman, *and* a pastor. And, also like Paul, I viewed all of these as callings from God.

We must dispel the myth that a commitment to Christ means you have to become a pastor or a missionary. That's not the case. Work done for a church or a church organization doesn't make anyone any more holy or spiritual than those whose work is done at a factory or in an office downtown or in a private studio. Our place or type of work doesn't matter to God. What *does* matter to Him is being in His will (Romans 12:2). We should approach our vocation, whether as a painter or a plumber, as a soldier or a mechanic, as a teacher or a "techie," not just merely as a job but as a calling—a special calling from God.

Being an Ambassador at Work

I first met "Ambassador" Jule in a Chicago hotel when he and I were both entering an elevator at the same time. Jule was in the area for a business meeting, and Elizabeth and I were on our way to a speaking seminar. We exchanged pleasantries as the elevator descended to the hotel lobby. Later that evening, Jule came to our dinner table and reintroduced himself after seeing my wife and me praying before eating our dinner. This "chance" encounter has developed into a wonderful friendship that's continued now for several years.

Jule is truly an ambassador for Christ at his work. He is very vocal about his faith. He leads a lunchtime Bible study and freely gives Bibles and Christian literature to anyone who is interested. Recently Jule sent me a book from a friend of his, entitled *Transforming Your Workplace for Christ*. (This shows you the kind of ambassador my friend Jule is!) In the introduction to the book, author William Nix made this statement:

> Your life can be marked by ministry. Be intentional about trying to transform your workplace for Christ....When you honor God by capturing your workplace for Christ, three things will happen:
>
> - You will experience fulfillment you have never before known.
> - Your coworkers will be drawn to you.
> - Your relationship with God will grow to an exciting new level.[35]

As a man after God's own heart, you, too, like my friend Jule and like William Nix, are to see yourself as Christ's ambassador at your workplace (2 Corinthians 5:20). An ambassador is one who represents another. An official ambassador to another country is a very special and influential person, and he or she must properly embody his country. Being Christ's ambassador is even more important. Therefore, you and I must properly represent Christ wherever we are and in whatever we do, *especially* at work. We represent the living God as we go about doing our job, whatever that may be.

Do you see yourself as Christ's ambassador? You should, because that's what you are. And what kind of ambassador are you? The apostle Paul commented on some individuals who were not being such good Christian ambassadors in the community: "We hear that some among you are idle. They are not busy; they are busybodies" (2 Thessalonians 3:11). Paul then added, "Such people we command and urge in the Lord Jesus Christ to settle down and earn the bread they eat" (verse 12).

Let's not be known as a busybody in the workplace! Let's be a good ambassador for Christ instead!

Glorifying God at Work

You and I as Christian men have a calling to serve and glorify God (1 Corinthians 10:31). The question is, where? The answer depends on our natural gifts and abilities as well as our spiritual enablements. Some men have a natural ability to work with their hands in factories or in construction or in art. Others excel at being creative and solving problems at a desk. There are many ways we can fulfill a vocation or calling. If you are struggling with knowing where you fit, you could ask for help from the leaders in your church or from a job or career counselor.

Whatever you do or are training to do, you should see it as an opportunity to honor and glorify God. What a difference it makes in your attitude to wake up every day knowing that you have the honor of serving the living God at your workplace and of being His ambassador while you are there!

Becoming a Winner

Thanks for staying with me as we looked to the Bible for God's perspective on work. You and I need to remember every day that work is the norm, that work is beneficial, that our work is a calling, that we are ambassadors for Christ on the job, and that our work is yet another way we can glorify God. There's more we can learn about being a man after God's own heart in our jobs, and we'll get to those principles in the next chapter. For now, I want to leave you with these words about becoming a winner.

A Winner

A Winner respects those who are superior to him and tries to learn something from them; a Loser resents those who are superior and rationalizes their achievements.

A Winner explains; a Loser explains away.

A Winner says, "Let's find a way"; a Loser says, "There is no way."

A Winner goes through a problem; a Loser tries to go around it.

A Winner says, "There should be a better way to do it"; a Loser says, "That's the way it's always been done here."

A Winner shows he's sorry by making up for it; a Loser says, "I'm sorry," but does the same thing next time.

A Winner knows what to fight for and what to compromise on; a Loser compromises on what he shouldn't, and fights for what isn't worth fighting about.

A Winner works harder than a loser, and has more time; a Loser is always "too busy" to do what is necessary.

A Winner is not afraid of losing; a Loser is secretly afraid of winning.

A Winner makes commitments; a Loser makes promises.[36]

*Y**ou have a choice between two attitudes as you go to work. You can go with an attitude of* taking from *your work whatever is needed for your own well-being. This attitude perceives the organization and its people as being there to serve you. Or you can go to work with the attitude that says, "What can I* put into *this organization or job?"*

—Jim George

12
A Heart That Glorifies God at Work

Part I

Whatever you do, whether in word or deed,
do it all in the name of the Lord Jesus.

—COLOSSIANS 3:17

It's been a while since we talked about our hero, King David. The whole premise of this book is that David was a man after God's own heart, a man who did God's will. David's desire in life was to obey God, but he didn't always come through. In this chapter, we're going to look at one of those times when David's spirit was willing...but the body was weak (Matthew 26:41).

The Pitfalls That Lead to Failure

In the times that David failed, we are usually able to figure out what caused the problem. For example, let's look at what happened when David committed adultery with Bathsheba, and see what we can learn from David's mistakes.

David was idle—Back in David's day, warfare was a seasonal thing. Battles were fought during good weather, usually from spring through the fall. As we pick up our narrative, we see this to be the case:

> In the spring, at the time when kings go off to war, David *sent Joab* out with the king's men and the whole Israelite army. They destroyed the Ammonites and besieged Rabbah. But *David remained* in Jerusalem (2 Samuel 11:1, emphases added).

Rather than join his men on the battlefront, David decided to stay home.

David was sensuous—I'm sure you've heard the saying, "An idle mind is the devil's workshop." Well, it appears that David's idleness contributed to a tragic episode in his life. As we noted, David wasn't where he was supposed to be. As king, his job was to lead his army into battle. Instead, he stayed behind. And, in an episode marked by carnality and sensuousness, we see the consequence of David's idleness.

> One evening David got up from his bed and walked around on the roof of the palace. From the roof he saw a woman bathing. The woman was very beautiful, and David sent someone to find out about her.... Then David sent messengers to get her...[and] he slept with her.... The woman conceived and sent word to David, saying, "I am pregnant" (2 Samuel 11:2-5).

David dishonored God—David wouldn't have gotten into this trouble if he had been on the job, leading his army. As a result, a woman was defiled and her husband was purposefully allowed to be killed in battle (2 Samuel 11:14-15). God was in no way honored by these terrible acts. In fact, the prophet Nathan said David's actions brought about the opposite results: "By this deed you have given occasion to the enemies of the LORD to blaspheme" (1 Samuel 12:14, NASB). With Nathan's rebuke, David realized and acknowledged that his sin was against God. Yes, others were affected, but David's actions ultimately dishonored God and His reputation before the unbelieving world. David knew that his sinful actions were directed toward a holy God when he remorsefully acknowledged, "I have sinned against the LORD" (2 Samuel 12:13).

This sordid example from David's life teaches us what to beware of—idleness, wrongful sensuousness, and dishonoring our Lord. As Colossians 3:17 says, we are to glorify God in whatever we do. Friend, as Christians, you and I represent Jesus Christ wherever we are—including our workplace. When we don't represent Him properly, we, like David, dishonor God and cause His name to be blasphemed.

If you're like most men, you will spend a good part of your life on the job. Therefore, you must make your workplace a platform for honoring God and causing His name to be praised. Here are five ways you can glorify God at work.

The Principles That Lead to Success

Principle #1: Be Diligent

Through his years of service, the apostle Paul discipled and trained many young men. One in particular was Timothy. We first meet Timothy in Acts 16:1 as a young man just entering the ministry. Then some 15 years later, we again meet Timothy, who by this time is the pastor of the church in Ephesus.

When Paul wrote to Timothy about his pastoral duties, he said, "Do your best to present yourself to God as one approved, a workman who does not need to be ashamed" (2 Timothy 2:15). In other words, Timothy was to make every effort to do his best so that he wouldn't have cause to be ashamed—not before his mentor, Paul, but before God, whom Timothy was really serving. Timothy was asked to be diligent at what he was called to do—preach and teach—so as not to shame the Lord.

Friend, God is asking you and me to develop that same heart of diligence and to be the best at what we do, too. Why? Here are a number of reasons:

- We give God glory *when* we do our best.
- We represent the Lord Jesus, *therefore* we do our best.
- We serve the Lord and not men, *so* we do our best.
- We provide a living model of our risen Savior *while* we do our best.
- We provide for our family *as* we do our best.

Over the years I've had the opportunity to visit India 15 times for ministry purposes. India is a fascinating and unique country with a great mass of people who need Jesus Christ. With a deep interest in India, my eye was drawn to this story that speaks of the diligence God is calling us to.

A missionary from India told about an army officer who stopped to have his shoes shined by a poor Indian boy on the street. The lad launched into his task with such enthusiasm and vigor that the man was utterly amazed. Instead of an ordinary, slipshod performance with all-too-eagerly outstretched hand for a tip, the boy worked diligently until the leather sparkled with a brilliant luster.

The officer asked, "Why are you taking so much time to polish my boots?"

"Well, sir," was the reply, "last week Jesus came into my heart and now I belong to Him. Since then, every time I shine someone's shoes, I keep thinking they're His, so I do the very best I can. I want Him to be pleased!"

Is the diligence this small boy demonstrated true of what you do as well? Are you willing to go so far as to shine shoes to the glory of God and please the One who died in your place? Because of what Christ has done for you and me, how can we do less than diligently give Him our best?

Principle #2: Be a Servant

I mentioned earlier that I once worked as a salesman. While in that position, I was asked to participate in a management training program at the corporate office of the pharmaceutical company I worked for. In the meetings, I was placed in a group with other aspiring managers. We were given a scenario and then asked to solve the problem. If you've ever been in this type of setting, you can visualize the scene as each of us attempted to demonstrate to the bosses that we were superior management material!

I'm not saying this exercise was bad; aspiring managers do need to learn to work with others to solve problems and assume leadership. But at the same time, I'm saying that we as Christian workers should go a step further and seek to excel at our job at all times—not just when the bosses are looking! As Christians, we are to approach *everything* in life as a servant, including business, management, or whatever kind of work we do. And I believe Jesus gives us guidance in this matter of servanthood.

Jesus, the Model Servant—The Lord Jesus Himself models the kinds of servants we ought to be. A week or so before His death, Jesus and His disciples were on their way up to Jerusalem.

During this journey two of His disciples, James and John, asked for positions of preeminence in the kingdom. Hear Jesus' reply:

> You know that the rulers of the Gentiles lord it over them, and their high officials exercise authority over them. Not so with you. Instead, whoever wants to become great among you must be your servant, and whoever wants to be first must be your slave—just as the Son of Man did not come to be served, but to serve, and to give his life as a ransom for many (Matthew 20:25-28).

Do you want to be great—in a good sense, that is? True leadership is not determined by dominance or seeking preeminence. Jesus was the greatest leader of all time...and yet He was a servant to all.

Following Jesus' example—Why not follow Jesus' example by being a servant to those whom you work with? (And don't forget—serving others is one of the marks of a godly man.) Here are a few suggestions for becoming a servant at work:

- Go with a servant's attitude
- Go to promote others
- Go to praise others
- Go to encourage others
- Go to ask, not tell
- Go to give, not take

You have a choice between two attitudes on the job. You can go with an attitude of *taking from* your work whatever is needed for your own well-being. This attitude perceives the organization and its people as existing to serve you. Or you can go to work with the attitude that says, "What can I *put into* this organization or job?" This better attitude seeks to make the organization better—cultivating a better work environment in which others are helped to live better and more satisfying lives. Bettering the lives of others is the role of a servant.

Principle #3: Be a Learner

Remember the epitaph on the scientist's tombstone in chapter 1—"He Died Learning"? Well, friend, that should be our motto as well. You and I should die learning. Unfortunately, many men have this backwards. Their motto is, "I would rather die than learn!" They disliked high school and couldn't wait for graduation so they could get on with "real life." Or, they exerted only what effort was necessary in order to get by. And today they have limited career options because they are not continuing their learning.

Now, I want to be quick to admit that I know many a man who has made it to the top levels of his firm or factory with only a minimum of formal education. I'm sure you could name a few men like this as well. (You may even be one of these self-made men yourself.) But if you look more closely at these men, you'll find that each one has continued his education—maybe not in a formal way, but informally. In other words, he has continued to learn on his own, and that is the reason for his progress. That's what I mean by being a learner. Learning isn't limited to schools and textbooks! Learning has to do with ongoing development of some kind. I see learning this way:

- Learning is a state of mind, an attitude.
- Learning is progressive—it builds upon itself.
- Learning is not dependent on your IQ.

- Learning does not distinguish between nationalities.
- Learning does not require a formal classroom education.
- Learning does not always offer a degree.
- Learning does not require a degree.
- Learning is commanded in the Bible (2 Peter 3:18).
- Learning is a man after God's own heart's way of life.

Let me again remind you that we are talking about glorifying God in our work. We've discussed diligence. We've also discussed *doing* our best. And learning is a part of *being* the best. As you learn, you will enable yourself to *do* your best and *be* the best.

Here are a few simple suggestions for continuing your learning:

Learn to read or to read better—Most men read very little...or not at all. In fact, surveys show that only about 5 percent of all Christian books are bought by men, and this percentage figure is down from 15 percent just ten years ago. Brother, if this is true, we are heading in the wrong direction when it comes to reading! Reading is the window to all learning. Reading exposes us to the world and to the knowledge and experiences of others. So how can we become better readers?

The best way to become a better reader is to read, read, and read some more! Like any other skill (or passion), over time, reading will make you a better reader. I've known men who hadn't read a book in years! But once they understood the importance of reading, some of them set a goal to read one book a month. (This may not sound like much of a feat to an avid reader, but for many men this would be a gigantic accomplishment!)

When the godly men at my church started helping me in my desire to be a man after God's own heart, I noticed they were always reading. Wanting to grow and wanting to emulate them, I asked for suggestions on what I should read. You can do the same. Why not ask the leaders in your church for a book list so you, too, can begin your own journey to leadership? It's been said, "A reader is a leader, and a leader is a reader."

And don't forget—the first book you should want to read is the Bible. Read it a little at a time from cover to cover, over and over, for the rest of your life. (For help on this, see the reading schedule in the back.)

Learn to ask questions—Not just any questions, but the right questions—questions that will expand your understanding of the subject at hand. Remember that you are a learner. That means that everyone has something to teach you. Approach every person on and off the job as your teacher. They are an expert on *something*. Find out what that something is, and then learn it from them. There's no such thing as a dumb question, so don't be afraid to ask questions. A question never asked is information never learned. Ask questions...and you just might learn something of great benefit to you.

Learn from the experiences of others—It's also been said that the person who depends upon his own experiences has relatively little material to work with. So I repeat, ask questions and glean from the experiences of anyone who is willing to teach you. Unfortunately, you can't pose questions of the great people of the past, but you *can* read their biographies. You can learn from their successes, and you can avoid their mistakes. And (again) don't forget your Bible. The Bible is the best of all books for learning from the experiences of others. (Just think how much we've already learned from the successes...and mistakes...of David!) The Bible should be your primary textbook for life, and for learning.

Learn to stretch yourself—At this time in your life and career, you may be becoming somewhat comfortable with your level of knowledge and job performance. Maybe you're looking at your position in the company and sitting back and feeling pretty proud of how far you've come. Why, it wasn't too many years ago that you started at an entry-level position, and now you feel ready to kick back and put your life on cruise control. Or, as one man so aptly put it, "you're sliding for home." I pray that's not the case with you. I pray you will never stop learning. To ensure that you continue to learn, take this "self-examination" every day:

- Ask yourself, "What new thing can I learn *today?*"
- Ask yourself, "Who can I learn from *today?*"
- Ask yourself, "How can I be stretched in some aspect of my job or life *today?*"
- Ask yourself, "Is there some type of training I need for my present job or in preparation for the next one?"

I'm chuckling as I write this, because in both pharmacy school and in seminary, I had professors who gave a test every day! And those were the teachers who stretched me the most...and the classes where I learned the most. I hope this list of daily self-examination questions will help you to stretch yourself!

One of my favorite generals of World War II is Douglas MacArthur. He was a no-nonsense soldier who asked a lot of himself and of his men. This is what he said about life and learning:

> Life is a lively process of becoming. If you haven't added to your interests during the past year, if you are thinking the same thoughts, relating the same personal experiences, having the same predictable reactions—*rigor mortis* of the personality has set in.[37]

For your information, *rigor mortis* is what happens to your body when you die! Don't allow this epitaph to be written about you:

Here lies __________.

He stopped learning at age _____.

He died in ignorance these many years later.

After taking to heart all that we've learned about diligence, servanthood, and learning, may *this* epitaph be yours as you seek to glorify God:

(Your name) died learning...

...for the glory of God!

What we need is a work ethic which is informed by God's Word and religiously lived out in the workplace and the church....how we work not only reveals who *we are, but determines* what *we are.*[38]

—Kent Hughes

13
A Heart That Glorifies God at Work

Part II

Whatever you do, work at it with all your heart, as working for the Lord, not for men....It is the Lord Christ you are serving.

—COLOSSIANS 3:23-24

I have a passion for studying and teaching about the lives of the godly men of the Bible. These men show us what it means to be a man after God's own heart. I love reading about Paul (as you can probably tell). He was a man after God's own heart. And I love learning about the life of David, the "original" man after God's own heart. But in the course of teaching a Bible class on the couples of the Bible, I met yet another man who has become a favorite: Boaz.

No, Boaz wasn't a king.

No, Boaz wasn't an apostle.

Boaz was more or less an ordinary guy, a guy more like you and me who got up every day and went to his job. He was a hardworking landowner who became Ruth's husband...and David's great-grandfather. (Ah, now we've discovered the gene pool of David! His great-grandfather, too, was a man after

God's own heart!) Note well this list of the virtues exhibited by Boaz's sterling life and work habits. He was:

- *Diligent*—Boaz is described as "a man of standing" (Ruth 2:1), and in the book of Ruth, we see him carefully and thoughtfully overseeing his property.
- *Friendly*—Boaz greeted his workers with warmth, and even welcomed the stranger named Ruth (2:4,8).
- *Merciful*—Noticing Ruth at work in his field, Boaz asked about her situation and acted on her behalf (2:7).
- *Godly*—Boaz asked Jehovah to bless Ruth in return for her care for Naomi, her widowed mother-in-law (2:12).
- *Encouraging*—Boaz pointed out Ruth's strong qualities and spoke of them to cheer her on (2:12; 3:11).
- *Generous*—Although Ruth needed food and was willing to work for it, Boaz gave her extra grain from his crops (2:15).
- *Kind*—When Ruth reported the considerate ways of Boaz, Naomi thanked God for His kindness shown to both of them through Boaz (2:20).
- *Discreet*—Boaz exhibited wise discretion by sending Ruth home from the threshing floor before daylight (3:14).
- *Faithful*—Following through on his promise to Ruth, Boaz "went to court" to clear the way to marry her (4:1-12).

The principles we've discussed regarding our work—being diligent, being a servant, being a learner—are most definitely lived out in Boaz. You don't become "a man of standing"—or a man after God's own heart—unless you're applying these principles!

It's good to see Boaz's example, isn't it? Now let's look at two more principles for glorifying God on the job.

Principle #4: Be Content

Contentment seems to be a lost virtue. We live in a restless society. The TV commercial blares, "You need this car!" The billboard beckons, "You need a vacation in the Caribbean!" Our affluent society, too, has programmed us to be discontent with what we have and covet what we don't have.

Now, you may be thinking, *Didn't Jim just tell me to be discontent with myself? Didn't he say I must never be satisfied with my status but should always be training, learning, and growing?* Yes, I did. But remember the context of my exhortation: *glorifying God at your job.* Discontentment for the glory of God differs from discontentment for your own glory or greed. In his little book entitled *The Rare Jewel of Christian Contentment*, the English Puritan Jeremiah Burroughs explained it this way:

> It may be said of one who is contented in a Christian way that he is the most contented man in the world, and yet the most unsatisfied man in the world; these two together must needs be mysterious.[39]

Paul's philosophy of contentment—The apostle Paul gives us words to live by when it comes to contentment. There's no doubt Paul was a great man. He was the human architect of much of our understanding of Christianity. He had what we could refer to as "places to go and people to meet." He was one of those "unsatisfied" Christians that Jeremiah Burroughs wrote about in the above-mentioned quote. Paul loved to travel and spread the gospel, yet God placed him in prison several times. That must have been hard, a human dynamo sitting in a dungeon! Yet while sitting in shackles, Paul wrote many of the letters that became books in our Bible. How thankful you and I should be that God arranged for Paul to have time to sit and think and write.

During one such "prison assignment," Paul wrote to his friends in the town of Philippi. He wanted to thank them for the gifts they sent to him while he was in prison. But he also wanted them to know that even if they hadn't been able to send him a gift, that was OK. He was perfectly content:

> I have learned to be content whatever the circumstances. I know what it is to be in need, and I know what it is to have plenty. I have learned the secret of being content in any and every situation (Philippians 4:11-12).

How could Paul write this? How could Paul be content? He's in prison, possibly facing execution! The answer is one we should remember for ourselves: Paul was content because *his contentment was based on trust*—a trust in the only One who could provide for him and strengthen him (Philippians 4:13).

Paul's contentment was not based on *provision*. It was based on a person—the *Person* of Jesus Christ. He ended his letter to his Philippian friends with this word of confidence: "My God will meet all your needs according to his glorious riches in Christ Jesus" (Philippians 4:19). Brother in Christ, this should be our philosophy on contentment as well. If God can and will and does provide for all our needs, then we should be content. That's biblical contentment! That's contentment God's way!

Paul's further advice on contentment—Friend, if you are not content with your job, Paul has a further word of advice for you in 1 Corinthians 7. His basic advice here is that our contentment is to be based on our *position* in Christ, not our personal *predicament*.

If you are discontent with your job, then you probably aren't overly excited with your work. And maybe you're able to "fake it" at work now. But be assured—your discontent will affect your performance. And ultimately, this kind of heart and behavior dishonors God. I suggest that you continually ask yourself these questions about your job...and your heart!

1. *Why am I here in this job?* If you sense your job is God's calling, you will see your job as a ministry and your work as a living sacrifice, "holy and pleasing to God" (Romans 12:1).

2. *For whom am I working?* Are you working for God or for men? When you serve God, you are free to serve others (Principle #2) no matter how unreasonable or thankless they are.

3. *What am I working for?* Money? Prestige? Power? If you are working for any of these, you will never be content. But if you can truly say, "I am working for the glory and the will of God," then you will be content.

4. *With whom am I working?* Every person at your workplace is an eternal soul. Each one will spend eternity either in the presence of God or separated from Him. You should be aware of every person at work and take every opportunity to model and testify to the reality of Jesus Christ through your life. Just think...you may be the only Christian some unbelievers know. That makes your job a mission field.

5. *Where am I working?* It is no accident that you work where you do. Ask God to open your eyes to the significance of the place where you are employed. What does God want to accomplish through you in that place?

Brother, whatever you do, don't spend your life in misery because you're discontent with your job. Contentment is yours when you remember...

- *why* you work—to please God
- *who* you work for—for God
- *what* you are working for—for God's glory
- *who* you are working with—potential members of God's kingdom
- *where* you are working—the center of God's will

Principle #5: Be a Model of Excellence

Excellence is one of my favorite words. I like the way it sounds, and I like the qualities it calls to mind. One writer defined *excellence* as "the maximum exercise of one's gifts and abilities within the range of the responsibilities given by God."[40] Don't you think you and I would glorify God if we lived out this definition on our jobs? It's a goal of mine...and I trust a goal of yours as well!

The question then becomes, How can you and I exercise this kind of excellence in all that we do? When it comes to our work, author and teacher Chuck Swindoll speaks of building a platform that rests on six pillars of excellence. He lists these pillars as integrity, faithfulness, punctuality, quality workmanship, a pleasant attitude, and enthusiasm. Let's take a few minutes to look at these essentials for excellence one by one so that we can better model true excellence on the job.

Integrity—*Integrity* is defined as being of sound moral principle, uprightness, honesty, and sincerity. Of all the people in the workforce, we as men of God should be men of integrity. Integrity should be the hallmark of our business life. Like Daniel, yet another man after God's own heart, there should be nothing dishonest that can be observed by others in our business practices. Instead, we, like Daniel, should be found "trustworthy and neither corrupt nor negligent" (Daniel 6:4).

Faithfulness—Faithfulness is part of the fruit of the Spirit (Galatians 5:22). When a faithful person says he's going to do something or be somewhere, he does it. David exhibited this kind of faithfulness when he fulfilled his promise to protect Jonathan's son (Mephibosheth) after Jonathan's death (2 Samuel 9:1-13). Don't make any promises that you can't or won't keep, and don't expect God's blessings on a life of unfaithfulness. (And don't expect a pay raise either!)

Punctuality—I'm sure you've been in meetings that were held up because everyone had to wait on that last person to arrive before they could get started. And as a result, time, energy, and momentum were lost. Don't let this late person be you. Start early. Make sure people are never waiting on you.

Quality workmanship—There was a time when quality workmanship was the rule and not the exception. Now it's the exception and not the rule. As a worker for Jesus Christ, we should want to produce quality workmanship. The next time you're tempted to cut corners, give a little less effort, or stop short of your maximum effort, remember that your workmanship is your offering to Jesus. Is your offering worthy?

> Whatever you do, work at it with all your heart, as working for the Lord, not for men, since you know that you will receive an inheritance from the Lord as a reward. It is the Lord Christ you are serving (Colossians 3:23-24).

A pleasant attitude—One of my two sons-in-law is a Navy submariner. You can imagine how much complaining goes on during the sub's three-to-six-month deployments! Paul tells me that he stands out from most of the crew simply because he tries to have a pleasant attitude and always stays positive about their mission. We as employees (of Christ) must resist the temptation to complain and grumble. To complain about anything, including our job, is seen as an accusation against God, as one writer notes:

> Complaining...questions God's wisdom and God's good judgment. God has always equated complaining with unbelief...[because] to complain is to doubt God. It is the same thing as suggesting that God really doesn't know what He's doing.[41]

Enthusiasm—*Enthusiasm* literally means "to be inspired or possessed by God." We could even use the word *impassioned.* How impassioned are you about your work? Do you approach each workday with an...

- eagerness to model Christ before a watching world?
- eagerness to contribute your energies to the success of your company or business?
- eagerness to contribute one more day's wages to the well-being of your family?
- eagerness to declare the praises of Him who called you out of darkness into His wonderful light?

Here's how Dr. Swindoll wrapped up his words about these six pillars of excellence: "Hire such a person and it will only be a matter of time before business will improve...people will be impressed...and Christianity will begin to seem important."[42]

And I would add, God will be glorified—which, my friend, is our whole reason for being.

Putting God's Principles into Practice

Have you noticed we've spent three chapters of this book dealing with our work life? This may seem like a lot, but it's not, when you consider that your job is where you spend at least a third of each day in terms of *actual* hours, and half of your day in terms of *waking* hours. (Either way, that's a lot of your life!)

In light of that, we can be grateful that the Bible contains so many principles about work. And I hope our study of some of these principles has helped you to view your job in a new light—*His* light. Your job, no matter what it is, is a high calling from God, and you should view it as important because it provides you with yet another opportunity to glorify Him daily. With that in mind, let's take this challenge to heart:

> What we need is a work ethic which is informed by God's Word and religiously lived out in the workplace and the church. The reason this is so important is that most of us spend eight to ten hours of our sixteen waking hours at work five or six days a week. So how we work not only reveals *who* we are, but determines *what* we are.[43]

Are you ready to approach your work differently? With an ethic built on diligence, servanthood, contentment, and excellence, all of which will glorify God? May your work ethic cause you, like Boaz, to be known by all as a man of influence and integrity in your community.

I love Thy kingdom, Lord,
The house of Thine abode,
The Church our blest Redeemer saved
With His own precious blood.

For her my tears shall fall,
For her my prayers ascend;
To her my cares and toils be given
Till toils and cares shall end.[44]

—TIMOTHY DWIGHT

14
A Heart That Loves the Church

Let us consider how we may spur one another on toward love and good deeds. Let us not give up meeting together.

—HEBREWS 10:24-25

Who is your favorite author? Maybe it's someone who is remembered for only one book. Or maybe it's John Wesley...or Charles Haddon Spurgeon...or someone else from long ago who produced mountains of writings. Or perhaps your favorite author is more contemporary, such as the prolific writer C. S. Lewis. Or, even more current authors such as Charles Swindoll, Max Lucado, or John MacArthur (at last count, each of these men have written many dozens of books).

Yet another prolific writer is the apostle Paul. He wrote more books in the New Testament than any other author.

Apart from our Lord Jesus Christ, the foremost figure in the history of Christianity is the apostle Paul. His personality, his writings, his preaching—all guided by the power of the Holy Spirit—have helped spread the Christian faith to the ends of the earth. I've heard that the library at Harvard Divinity School contains more than 2,000 volumes dealing with the life and letters of this great apostle. In addition, the library contains thousands of commentaries in which Paul's teachings occupy an important place. Based on the works that have been written about Paul and his writings, and the fact that he wrote 13 books of the New Testament, we can conclude that here is a man whose writings are worthy of our serious attention...especially when it comes to recognizing the importance of the church, the body of Christ!

Understanding the Importance of the Church

Aside from Paul's consistent theme of salvation by grace through faith (see, for example, Ephesians 2:8-9 and Titus 3:5), his teachings on the church are one of the most dominant subjects in his writing. That should serve as a clue that you and I, as men after God's own heart and as men who desire to fulfill all of God's will, ought to heed Paul's heartfelt teachings on this most important subject. If God inspired Paul to say so much about the church, then clearly the church is important to God, and likewise, it should be important to us. Here's a sampling of what Paul taught about the church in just one of his 13 letters, the book of Ephesians:

- the church is headed by Christ (Ephesians 1:22)
- the church is Christ's body (1:23)
- the church is to show forth the wisdom of God (3:10)
- the church is subject to Christ (5:24)
- Christ loved and died for the church (5:25)

- Christ feeds and cares for His church (5:29)
- we, as believers, are members of Christ's body, the church (5:30)

And there's much more Paul says about the church. Given this emphasis, we can see why the church—both worldwide and our local church—should be important to us. In fact, the church is a *priority* for a man after God's own heart!

Being a Member of Christ's Body

I can't imagine ever meeting *any* man who is not a member of *some* organization—be it for business or for pleasure. And we all know that organizations typically have standards for the members to follow—either voluntarily or through some type of enforcement. Dear friend, whether you understand it or not, as a believer in Jesus Christ, you are a member of Christ's body, the church. This membership gives you many incredible privileges, but it also means that you have many weighty responsibilities. You can't have one without the other.

The privileges of membership—I'm sure you've heard the slogan of one credit card company, which says, "Membership has its privileges." Well, our membership in the body of Christ has its privileges, too. In the book of Ephesians, Paul wrote about a few of the blessings of being a part of Christ's body, the church. (And please note that this list covers only the first 13 verses in Ephesians 1! There are many other "privileges" that your "membership" offers you!)

- You were chosen before the foundation of the world (verse 4).
- You were adopted as sons (verse 5).
- You have the forgiveness of sin (verse 7).

- You have been given an inheritance (verse 11).
- You were sealed in Christ by the Holy Spirit (verse 13).

The responsibilities of membership—While a credit card may give you privileges, it comes with responsibilities as well (like paying your bill each month!). Likewise, as a member of Christ's body, you have obligations—God asks you to fulfill your "membership duties." Here's a partial list of your responsibilities (note that these commitments come from just one chapter in the book of Ephesians—there are many more!):

- You are to live a life worthy of your calling (4:1).
- You are to be humble and gentle, patiently bearing with others in love (4:2).
- You are to be trained by your church leaders for works of service (4:12).
- You are to become mature, attaining to the whole measure of the fullness of Christ (4:13).
- You are to be made new in the attitude of your mind (4:23).
- You are to put on the new self, created to be like God in true righteousness and holiness (4:24).
- You are to speak the truth (4:25).
- You are to be honest in all your dealings (4:28).
- You are to speak only words that benefit your listeners (4:29).
- You are to get rid of all bitterness, wrath, anger, brawling, and slanderous speech, along with every form of malice (4:31).
- You are to be kind and compassionate and forgiving (4:32).

That's quite a list, isn't it? We can't read something like this and not wonder how we are doing in fulfilling some of these responsibilities. We have our work cut out for us, don't we? Fortunately for us, God is gracious and patient and doesn't revoke our membership in Christ's body when we fail to live up to our responsibilities. Why don't we stop for a minute and praise God for His mercy? Let's thank Him for His graciousness toward us.

As we move on, let's keep in mind that indeed, membership has its privileges, and with those privileges comes responsibility. You can't have one without the other.

Developing a Passion for the Church

For many years I lived a lukewarm form of Christianity with little or no involvement in a local church. Call it drifting, call it distraction, call it enamorment with the things of the world, or even sin. Whatever you call it, my heart was not fixed on or consumed with the things of the Lord. Then, by God's grace, I was awakened to realize the crucial place my local church had in my life.

My return to the church began when I met a dynamic Christian man while on the job. God used that one man to ignite within me a new passion for the Lord, for His Word, and for going to church. Then when I began attending church again, some godly men began to disciple me and help me grow. They began to teach me about the significance of the church in God's program and the part I needed to play.

And the results were literally life-changing, for both me and my family. We gained many new friends who care about us and help us. Our children made wonderful friends as well. We came to know the joy and fulfillment that comes from being an active part of God's work. And we grew in spiritual maturity to the point where we are active in serving Christ and others.

Our participation in church gave us direction, meaning, and purpose.

Church can do that for your family, too. If you're not actively involved, Christ is calling you to be so. If you're not sure whether you're in the right church, determine to find the best church for your family. (I know that can be difficult—it took us several months.) Determine to be faithful. Determine to be active. Determine to grow. Developing a passion for the church is a matter of obedience...obedience that leads to manifold blessings. So, determine to be obedient!

Becoming a More Useful Member

You may already be actively involved in your local church. (This is as it should be, and I commend you for this.) But, like the apostle Paul, I would exhort you "to do so more and more" (1 Thessalonians 4:10).

Here's a list of some ways that you can demonstrate to God, to the church family, and to your own family that you see the church as important in your life. Feel free to add some of your own ideas to this list.

Attend faithfully—Earlier we learned that one of the marks of a godly man is that he worships God regularly. If worshiping God and growing spiritually are priorities in your life, you will make room in your schedule to attend church on Sunday. You should also look for other opportunities for spiritual input, such as classes or seminars for men or couples. You and your family can never get too much input from God's Word! A wise man seeks wisdom (Proverbs 15:14), and that wisdom is available at your local church. Do you want to be the spiritual leader in your family? Then faithfully attend church with your family, and you will be well on your way to being the leader that God means for you to be.

Give generously—The Bible has a lot to say about money. In fact, Jesus spoke more about money than any other subject. Why? Not because the God of all creation needs our resources...which originally came from Him, anyway! But because we need to be careful about our heart attitude toward money, which can easily distract us from the real priorities in life.

It's been said that you can tell what a man's priorities are by looking at his checkbook. When you invest your "treasure" in God's church and God's people, you will have a much greater "heart" interest in the well-being of others. Why? Because "where your treasure is, there your heart will be also" (Matthew 6:21).

If you're not used to giving to the church, start like Elizabeth and I did. Start with where you are and with what you have. Start with giving to the church at the front end of each paycheck instead of the back end. Start by asking God to help you develop discernment about the ways you handle your money. Ask Him to reveal to you any areas of greed or selfishness in your life. Your goal is to give with a cheerful heart. As Paul wrote, "Remember this: Whoever sows sparingly will also reap sparingly, and whoever sows generously will also reap generously...for God loves a cheerful giver" (2 Corinthians 9:6-7).

Pray regularly—The apostle Paul called the men of the church to be men of prayer (1 Timothy 2:1-8). He often asked his readers to "pray in the Spirit on *all* occasions with *all* kinds of prayers and requests...[and to] be alert and *always* keep on praying for *all* the saints" (Ephesians 6:18, emphases added). My friend, as a man after God's own heart, you should pray regularly not only for your family, but also for your church and its leaders and ministries. Write out a prayer list for the people you know both in and out of the church, and then "pray continually" (1 Thessalonians 5:17).

Serve diligently—Remember again my deacon friend—the one who couldn't wait to get to church so he could serve the people there? His enthusiasm is a great example for us. Serving others requires no education or training. You can start serving in your church today! How? Some possibilities include…

- setting up chairs and tables for the next church social or meeting
- doing repairs at the church by using your mechanical or carpentry skills
- cleaning the sanctuary before and after the services
- greeting visitors on Sunday before the service

There are always opportunities available for serving somewhere in a church, and it's a great honor to serve our Lord. By committing ourselves to serving, we show that we are men after God's own heart.

I know we've covered a lot of ground in this chapter, and there's a lot to remember. But in a nutshell, it's enough for you to take steps to become an active and useful member of your church. Just be sure you don't fall into the trap of excusing yourself from service, as the unknown person in the following poem did.

I'll Go Where You Want Me to Go—Maybe

I'll go where You want me to go, dear Lord,
  Real service is what I desire.
I'll sing You a solo any time, dear Lord,
  Just don't ask me to sing in the choir.

I'll do what You want me to do, dear Lord,
  I like to see things come to pass.
But don't ask me to teach boys and girls,
    O Lord.
  I'd rather just stay in my class.

I'll do what You want me to do, dear Lord,
  I yearn for Thy kingdom to thrive.
I'll give You my nickels and dimes, dear Lord.
  But please don't ask me to tithe.

I'll go where You want me to go, dear Lord,
  I'll say what You want me to say;
I'm busy just now with myself, dear Lord,
  I'll help You some other day. [45]

S*tart where you are—do* anything *you can do, and do* everything *you can do, until you find* something *you must do! That* something *is probably your spiritual gift.*

—JIM GEORGE

15
A Heart That Serves the Church

Now to each one the manifestation of the Spirit is given for the common good.

—1 CORINTHIANS 12:7

There are many ways that a man after God's own heart can serve in his local church. With that in mind, I'd like to share my version of something I ran across in my reading. This list shows us some ways you and I can serve in our church:

Have phone . . . . will call.
Have pen . . . . will write.
Have desire . . . . will come.
Have car . . . . will bring.
Have money . . . . will give.
Have voice . . . . will sing.
Have concern . . . . will pray.
Have love . . . . will praise.
Have gifts . . . . will serve.

Not very earth-shattering, is it? And yet these are just a few of the simple things you and I can do that mean so much to others in the church.

For the rest of this chapter, I want to zero in on the last item on this "to do" list: "Have gifts...will serve."

Understanding Spiritual Gifts

No study of the church or of your heart as a man after God would be complete without at least some mention of spiritual gifts. A spiritual gift is a spiritual ability given to believers by God and empowered by the Holy Spirit for the purpose of ministering to others in the body of Christ, the church. God wants to work through you and me as we discover, develop, and use our spiritual gifts to minister to the other members of His church.

Defining Spiritual Gifts

As soon as you can, take a few minutes to read the three most important passages in the Bible on the subject of spiritual gifts: Romans 12:4-8, 1 Corinthians 12:1-31, and 1 Peter 4:10-11. Here are some basic principles these passages teach in regard to spiritual gifts:

- Spiritual gifts are an important aspect of Paul's teaching (1 Corinthians 12:1).
- Their source is the Holy Spirit (1 Corinthians 12:11).
- They are not natural abilities (1 Corinthians 12:4).
- There are no greater or lesser gifts (1 Corinthians 12:15-27).
- They are for the church's benefit (1 Corinthians 12:11; 1 Peter 4:10).

Spiritual gifts are given to us by God for the benefit of others in the church. We can't mail in or phone in the use of our spiritual gifts. And we can't delegate the use of our gifts. We must be physically involved for our gifts to be of use to others. That's why it's so important for us to be actively involved in a local church.

Can you imagine what a church would be like if every member made use of his or her spiritual gifts every time he or she went to church? What a blessing that would be for everyone! It would be a little bit of heaven on earth. And what a testimony that would be to a watching world, which would see Jesus Christ through our actions, rather than a group of bickering, self-centered, inactive believers.

Recognizing Your Spiritual Gifts

There are a variety of spiritual gifts. And it may take us a while to determine our area of giftedness and learn how to best minister to the other members of our church. Here are some suggestions for determining your area of giftedness:

Start where you are—Do *anything* you can do, and do *everything* you can do, until you find *something* you must do! That *something* is probably your spiritual gift.

This is what Elizabeth and I did when we first began attending church. We did *anything* and *everything* we could possibly do. It was such a joy to serve anybody and everybody in any way! And then, in time, as we allowed God to work through us, we began to find tasks that were ideally suited to us, which were our areas of giftedness.

Start with what you like—At the time of your salvation, God gave you spiritual abilities (1 Corinthians 12:11). These abilities are an inherent part of your Christian makeup. They are uniquely "you." And they are not exactly like anyone else's abilities.

As you grow and mature spiritually, these spiritual abilities will surface more and more as you have opportunities to serve. You will find that you have an interest and a passion to minister and serve in the areas where God has gifted you. So the best way to discover your area of giftedness is to do what you like to do or desire to do. That, and your spiritual growth, will help to confirm your spiritual gift.

Start asking others—Many times you won't recognize your spiritual giftedness. Why? Because what you are doing will seem to come naturally. Your actions will seem too easy, too effortless. That's because your area of spiritual giftedness is a channel through which the *Holy Spirit* works—it's not *you*, it's *Him!* This is hard to explain and hard to understand, and sometimes it's hard to recognize. But just keep on keeping on! And ask others what *they* see as your most effectual area of service. Their observations will probably indicate your area of giftedness.

Start with what God is blessing—God has given you spiritual abilities designed to bless others. When you are using your God-given gifts, others will be blessed in obvious ways. Also, your gifts will become more obvious as God blesses certain ministries you undertake. So if you are wondering what your gifts are, just take a look around to see what you are doing for the body of Christ that God is blessing.

(And P.S.—You will feel blessed as you obediently and humbly minister your gifts. Yours will be the joy of knowing that you are fulfilling your special role in the proper functioning of Christ's body, the church.)

Kicking It Up a Notch

My daughter Courtney is an aspiring chef. She's taken a few culinary classes, and, whenever time permits (she's a mother of three preschoolers!), Courtney watches the cooking channel. Knowing of her interest in cooking, I have occasionally stopped to watch the cooking channel myself (usually on the way to my favorite channel, the Weather Channel!).

While watching the cooking channel, I've encountered Chef Emeril. (Your wife will probably know who he is.) Every so often when this master chef wants to increase the difficulty of the recipe or try something a little more complicated or spicy, he says, "Let's kick it up a notch!"

Aspiring to Greater Use by God

Well, this is not the cooking channel (thank goodness!), but in relation to our spiritual service, I would like for us to "kick it up a notch." I would like to wrap up our discussion on service and spiritual gifts with a challenge from the apostle Paul himself. Paul wrote these words to his young disciple Timothy in relation to selecting leaders for the local church, and they apply to you and me as well:

> If anyone sets his heart on being an overseer,
> he desires a noble task (1 Timothy 3:1).

I like three things about this simple statement from Paul.

First, I like the words "If anyone." Did you notice that? Paul is not talking here about an elite, select group of people, but *anyone*—which includes men like you and me!

Second, I like the passion transmitted by Paul's words "sets his heart on." Paul is talking about a longing or an eagerness. Or, as a different translation of the Bible puts it in just one passionate word, "aspire" (NASB). He is talking about those who have a desire to lead in some way or at some level in the church.

And third, I like the affirmation offered by the words "a noble task," which can also be translated "a good work," "an excellent work," "an honorable ambition."

Summed up, Paul is saying it's OK—even desirable and right—for men like you and me to aspire to be a leader of some kind in our church. Such aspiration is not a bad thing. In fact, the "bad thing" just might be *not* aspiring to leadership. So, let's kick it up a notch! Let's set our hearts on discovering and developing and using our spiritual gifts...of pursuing a life of godliness...and see where that road leads us.

The Qualities for Usefulness to God

Paul then goes on to say that the person who has this aspiration is marked by certain qualities. That is, there are certain qualities required in those in positions of leadership in the local church. And those same qualities are to be pursued by all men who desire a more godly life.

You'll find a number of these qualities listed here (taken from 1 Timothy 3:1-7 and Titus 1:6-9). As you go through them one by one, stop and prayerfully ask God to fashion your life into a man after His own heart, a man who is...

Not given to drunkenness—Literally translated, this means "not given to wine or to be a drunkard."[46] This quality forbids excessive use of wine or other alcoholic beverages. Godliness and drunkenness are not compatible.

Not violent—This means "not a striker" (KJV), and speaks of not getting involved in brawls. A man of God refrains from being quick-tempered and quick-fisted. He keeps himself under control (Proverbs 29:11).

Not quarrelsome—A godly man will not participate in arguments. He is not a contentious person. Rather, his conversation is always full of grace (Colossians 4:5) and he is kind to all (2 Timothy 2:24).

Not a lover of money—This quality appears as one word in the original Greek text and literally means "not a silver lover." A love of money can become the root that nourishes all kinds of other sins (1 Timothy 6:10). A man pursuing godliness cannot be preoccupied with amassing material possessions.

While it's true that money is necessary to furnish our needs, we should not allow it to lead us to become greedy.

Not overbearing—This phrase is made up of two words that mean "self-pleasing, arrogant."[47] When you think of Jesus, do the words *stubborn and headstrong* come to mind? Quite the contrary! Like our Savior, we should strive to be a humble servant to all (Matthew 11:29).

Not quick-tempered—This quality, which is mentioned in Titus 1:7, has to do with controlling your temper. God's man doesn't "fly off the handle." He doesn't have a short fuse.

Not pursuing dishonest gain—If a man has a "love of money," he may end up resorting to dishonest gain in order to satisfy his greedy desires. God's man is careful not to get involved in anything that might appear to be dishonest or illegal. He will "avoid every kind of evil" (1 Thessalonians 5:22).

Just—This word from Titus 1:8 refers to the practical day-to-day uprightness of our lives. We are to do what is right and fair. We are to be men who are honest in our dealings with others. We are to be men of integrity.

Loving what is good—God's man has a passion for what is good and wholesome, whether in the books and magazines he reads, the movies and TV shows he watches, or the friendships and hobbies he cultivates.

These, then, are some of the qualities that are important in the life of a man who desires to lead in some capacity in the church.

Beginning the Journey

My Journey

You may be familiar with the saying that "every journey of a thousand miles begins with a first step." Well, my traveling friend, my first step toward growing in godliness and discovering my spiritual gifts was service. As I've already shared with you, when I finally got serious about being a Christian and became actively involved in my local church, I didn't have a clue what it meant to be a leader (and at that point in time, it didn't matter!). I was just happy to be back in the center of God's will, back at church, back with God's people, and back in God's Word. I was thrilled at the prospect of serving in any capacity in my church, so I made myself available for any and every opportunity to serve.

While I was serving, I was also growing spiritually. I attended church regularly, I sought out godly men to disciple me, I attended Bible training seminars, and I read my Bible and studied it diligently. I didn't understand much about spiritual gifts, ministry, or leadership. I just wanted to be faithful in what little I did understand. It was in the process of faithfully *serving* in my church that God gave me the privilege of *serving as a leader* in my church.

Your Journey

Like me, you might not be able to do much in the beginning. And, like me, you might not be quite sure what your spiritual gifts are. (In fact, you may sometimes wonder if God forgot to give a spiritual gift to you!) But God *has* gifted you, and you can begin making use of that giftedness by...

- serving faithfully where you are (1 Corinthians 4:2),
- continuing to grow spiritually (2 Peter 3:18),
- accepting greater challenges of service as God blesses you,
- aspiring to leadership (1 Timothy 3:1), and
- desiring to be godly (1 Timothy 3:1-7; Titus 1:6-9).

The journey is yours. You can choose to take the "high road"—the road of challenge and discipline and growth...or you can choose to take the "low road"—the road of nonchalance and ease and selfishness and mediocrity. But I guarantee you that choosing to journey on the high road of eagerly aspiring to godliness and leadership will bring far greater results and blessing to you and your family. Taking the high road does not promise that you will become a leader. But that's OK, for you will still have grown and matured and excelled simply because you aimed high. And, my friend, taking that road will mark you as a man after God's own heart.

If you feel uncertain about whether you can handle the journey, remember, as we learned earlier, a journey of a thousand miles begins with a first step. And a journey continues at only one step at a time—that is, at a pace that is realistic and manageable. All that's necessary is that we make sure we're headed in the right direction...and we can be sure that God will give us the stamina and strength for every step along the way.

Rise Up, O Men of God!

Rise up, O men of God!
Have done with lesser things;
Give heart and soul and mind and strength
To serve the King of kings.

Rise up, O men of God!
The Church for you doth wait,
Her strength unequal to her task:
Rise up, and make her great!

Lift high the cross of Christ!
Tread where His feet have trod:
As brothers of the Son of Man
Rise up, O men of God![48]

If you want to be a good witness *for Jesus Christ on your job, then be the very best* worker *on your job. People don't want to hear about Jesus Christ from a guy who is an average worker. But they will stand in line to talk to the very best worker in their company.*

—Bob Vernon

16
A Heart That Reaches Out

...you will be my witnesses...

—ACTS 1:8

Have you ever been a part of an event or meeting that had a long-lasting impact on your life? I have! For me it was an evening men's class at my church called "The True Masculine Role." The teacher was Bob Vernon. Bob is what we would definitely call a man's man. He's the kind of guy men would follow anywhere and, if prompted, do just about anything he asked. At the time that I was taking the class, Bob was a captain in the Los Angeles Police Department. Later Bob became the Assistant Chief of Police for the LAPD, and ultimately, he was a finalist for the chief's job.

One evening during the six-week class, Bob talked about being a witness on the job. He made a powerful statement I have not forgotten to this day: "If you want to be a good *witness* for Jesus Christ on your job, then be the very best *worker* on your job. People don't want to hear about Jesus Christ from a guy who is an average worker. But they will stand in line to talk to the very best worker in their company."

Bob was talking about being a missionary on the job—about the difference that diligence will make in earning the right to share about Jesus with others.

Earning the Right

Bob's challenge made a lasting impression on all of us in the class. And it points out yet another priority for us as men after God's own heart—that of evangelism. Jesus left His disciples—and us—with this command as He was preparing to return to heaven, "You will be my witnesses" (Acts 1:8). We are Christ's representatives here on earth, and we are called to live in such a way that the people around us can see God in our lives and are drawn toward Him.

If we do our work poorly, we can expect that unbelievers will not be attracted to God—in fact, they may even question whether Christianity is a good thing. As Bob Vernon said, hard work will earn you the right to talk about anything you want—your job, the reason for your "success" (which is Christ), and even your faith. It will pave the way for you to tell others of the motivation behind your "success"—Jesus Christ. When you are the best on the job, then your co-workers will come to you for answers—answers about work...and eventually, about life and its meaning.

Becoming a Neighbor

Another way we can earn the right to share about our faith in Christ is by being truly concerned for others. You may have heard the saying, "People don't care what you know until they know that you care." That's very true—our workmates must see us as approachable, caring, and friendly. In other words, they must see us as a neighbor.

"Who is my neighbor?" Jesus was asked this question by a religious leader who was seeking approval for his religious efforts. And Jesus answered that question by telling the story of the Good Samaritan (Luke 10:25-37)—the story of a man who showed genuine care even for someone he didn't know.

Before we can expect others to listen to what we might say about Christ, we need to build friendships with those whom we are in contact with on a regular basis. As you and I become better "neighbors," we earn the right to share about our Savior. And the story of the Good Samaritan contains eight principles for developing a heart that reaches out and for becoming the kind of neighbor others will listen to.

Developing a Heart That Reaches Out

Principle #1: Love takes the initiative (Luke 10:30-34)—Before Jesus began the story of the Good Samaritan, He condemned several nearby cities for their lack of hospitality and rejection of the gospel message. Then in the story itself, Jesus contrasted the *unloving actions* of a priest and a Levite (two groups of Jewish religious leaders) with the *loving actions* of a Samaritan (a person whom Jews considered an outcast because of his background). The two religious leaders had each moved to the other side of the road in order to avoid an encounter with a fellow Jew who had been beaten by robbers. Both most likely believed they had good reasons for neglecting this man in his hour of need. But it was obvious that he was badly wounded. They could have helped. They should have helped! But they didn't.

Then along came the Samaritan. What was his response? Jesus said the Samaritan "saw him [and] took pity on him. He went to him and bandaged his wounds" (verses 33-34). The

Good Samaritan saw…and he responded. He took the initiative by coming to the wounded man's aid.

You see, love is always looking for a place to show itself. Love is taking action. The priest and Levite demonstrated no love, for they did nothing. They took no action. Love always takes the initiative. In fact, this is exactly the kind of love God showed toward us when we were sinners:

> God so loved the world that he *gave* his one and only son, that whoever believes in him shall not perish but have eternal life (John 3:16, emphasis added).
>
> God *demonstrated* his own love for us in this: While we were still sinners, Christ died for us (Romans 5:8, emphasis added).

Aren't you thankful that God took the initiative and sent His Son to die for us? What a great example for you and me to follow with respect to those around us. Is there someone, some non-Christian you can think of right now, to whom you can demonstrate God's love this week?

Some years ago when my family and I were on our way to Singapore for a time of missions work, we passed through Taiwan so that I could visit a friend who had been a fellow student while I was in seminary. During our visit, my friend and I were talking about friendship evangelism, and he related this story to me.

Steve had met a Bible student whose father hated Christians and Christianity. This father also hated the fact that his son was attending a Bible school. To show his contempt, the father would meet his son at the door of the school at the end of each day and whip him with a stick all the way home. Eventually it came about that one of the faculty members discovered that the father liked tea. This teacher went to the father and asked to know how he prepared his tea, for he, too, was a tea drinker. As a result of that initiative and genuine interest, the father eventually waned in his dislike for Christians, became open to learning about the meaning of the gospel, and even stopped beating his son! Love takes the initiative.

Principle #2: Love the unlovely (Luke 10:33)—Let's think about the picture Jesus painted in His story about the Good Samaritan. While a Jewish traveler was on his way to his destination, he was mugged, beaten, robbed, and left for dead. We can be certain he was not a very lovely sight as he lay on the side of the road wounded, bleeding, and dying. He was definitely an "unlovely" person! Evidently the two religious leaders who passed him by on the road thought so too, as they sidestepped any contact with their fellow Jew by crossing the road and hastily going on their way.

But the Samaritan—better yet, the *Good* Samaritan (who was a non-Jew!)—stopped and ministered to this needy and suffering man. He showed love for the unlovely.

It's easy to love your friends and "lovely people." But Jesus shows us, by way of a story, that we need to love those who are not so lovely, and who may even hate us. We need to show that kind of love to our coworkers and our neighbors.

I remember well when Elizabeth and I first opened our home for a Bible study. People were encouraged to invite their non-Christian friends and workmates. One young man invited a certain girl from his work and, to his surprise, she came! Mary would not have made the cover of the latest fashion magazine. Her hair was a mess, and her dress was dirty and wrinkled. In fact, you probably would have wondered if she had slept in it. Mary definitely did not take care of herself or fit the profile of the others in the study. She was what some would label as "unlovely."

From the first night of the study, we endeavored to treat Mary with the same respect and attention as the other members of the group. After several weeks of attending the study, she said to me, "Since you didn't treat me as weird, I won't think of you as weird because you are a Christian."

Friend, some time later, Mary accepted Christ into her life! I share this story with humility and praise to God for His love. It would have been easy to ignore Mary because of her appearance. But God calls for you and me to love even the unlovely, and we can see the good result it had on Mary's life. I hope you'll be encouraged to make an effort, with God's help, to see past the externals of people you may be tempted to think of as unlovely. Seek to view each person for what he or she really is—a lost soul in need of a Savior. Seek to love the unlovely.

Principle #3: No impact without contact (Luke 10:33)—How much of an impact do you think the priest and Levite had on the wounded, half-dead traveler? None! But the Samaritan (better yet, the *Good* Samaritan) had an impact...because he had contact. He went out of his way to come alongside the man and bandage up his wounds.

Nicki is another soul God brought to our home. She was our mail carrier. Nicki was friendly, and our family got to know her as she made her daily rounds. She liked our neighborhood so much that she bought a house down the street from us. On occasion we talked with Nicki about religious matters. She was always cheerful and polite and seemed to enjoy listening. However, things never progressed beyond these friendly talks.

But there was more to Nicki's life than we knew. Her husband was an alcoholic. They split and he left, and things went from bad to worse when she invited a motorcycle gang leader to move in with her. Then Nicki had a baby. In time, she quit her job at the post office and we lost contact with her.

Months went by....and then we heard that Nicki had gone to the local park one night, killed her little girl, and then killed herself. Our family felt very badly about the tragedy. In hindsight, I wonder…were we too busy doing our own thing? What if we had continued our contact with her? Were we like the priest and Levite, walking by on the other side of the street? Did we forfeit our impact? Were we like the priest and Levite, somehow forfeiting our impact on Nicki's life by ceasing to have contact with her?

Brother, don't let this happen to you! Is there someone in your neighborhood or at work who is wounded and bleeding and in need of Christ's loving contact through you? Don't walk by on the other side of the street, or down the other hall at work, or on the other side of the parking lot!

Let's go back to the tea-drinking faculty member in Taiwan for a moment. Not only did he reach out to the Bible student's father, he also made friends with a local tea merchant. For two years he faithfully dropped by the man's store to have tea and to learn more about tea. One day when the teacher entered the store, the owner said, "You are different. It must be because you are a Christian."

Remember…no impact without contact!

Principle #4: Love requires a broken heart (Luke 10:33)—What did the Samaritan do when he spotted the dying man alongside the road? Jesus says that "he had pity on him." Another version of the Bible says "he felt compassion" (NASB). In other words, his heart went out to the wounded man. This is a reference to the Samaritan's emotions. Have you ever felt "sick to your stomach" over some issue or incident? Then you know how the Samaritan man felt about the wounded Jew. His heart was broken, and he did something about the situation. He took care of the dying man's needs.

Jesus experienced the same emotion when He came upon a funeral procession for the only son of a widow. The woman had already lost her husband and now she had lost her only son. And Jesus' heart went out to her (Luke 7:13). His heart was broken, and he did something about the situation—He raised the woman's son from the dead!

Is your heart broken over the spiritual needs of your neighbors and workmates? Or do you need an experience with someone like our Nicki? Never look with a calloused or fearful eye at those around you. Reaching others for Christ requires a broken heart. It requires a heart that desires to help those in need.

Principle #5: Witness both verbally and nonverbally—Have you noticed yet that the Samaritan didn't say a word to the wounded man? Read through the story for yourself. The Samaritan didn't have to say anything. His actions spoke volumes!

While going through my teaching files I found these words from a book entitled *Friendship Evangelism*. They have a powerful message for us:

> It is easy to talk about the love of God, but what convinces people of its reality is not your words alone, but also your way. If you demonstrate by the way you live and relate to others that the love of God has become a reality in your own experience, then you have something that is hard for people to walk away from. As someone has written, "The greatest proof of God's love is a life that needs His love to explain it."[49]

French philosopher Voltaire once said, "Show me your redeemed life and I'll believe in your redeemer." We tend to think of our witness as being verbal. But pointing people to Christ is not so much what you *say*, but what you *are!* You've probably heard that popular saying, "Don't talk the talk unless you can walk the walk." There's a need for your nonverbal witness to back up your verbal witness! To some people your life, your nonverbal witness, is the only Bible they will ever read. So...what message are you conveying?

Principle #6: Be flexible (Luke 10:33-35)—Why didn't the priest and the Levite stop to help the wounded traveler? We don't know for sure, but it's clear they didn't want to be inconvenienced in any way. They were on a journey, and didn't want to be interrupted.

Contrast their actions with those of the Samaritan. He, too, was going somewhere. The Bible says he came upon the wounded man "as he traveled." Another translation says he "was on a journey." No, the Samaritan wasn't looking for wounded Jews along the side of the road. But he saw one in need, and he was flexible. The Samaritan cared for the man on the spot. Not only that, he also set the man on his own donkey and took him to an inn where he continued his care of the wounded man until the next day. That's flexibility!

One day something similar happened to me. I was driving on a major city street in the Los Angeles area, and the road was absolutely jammed with cars. The traffic was moving slowly, and as a result, I was late for a meeting at the church. As I inched my way forward, I spotted a woman standing beside a stalled car on the median in the middle of the road. I pulled in behind her and learned that her car was out of gas. Well, I turned around, went to a gas station, got some gas, and inched my way back through the traffic to her car. As I left, I gave her my pastoral card and said, "If there's anything else I can do for you, let me know." She looked at the card and said, "Oh, I'm Jewish." Then I said, "That's no problem. If I can help in any way, give me a call."

One week later, Barbara called with a major problem in her family and asked for my help. Eventually she even came to church. Friend, you never know who the Lord is going to place in your path. Therefore it's important to take the time to be flexible. Treat each encounter as a divine encounter. Be flexible, and be blessed!

Principle #7: Be willing to sacrifice (Luke 10:34-35)—Friendship evangelism and being a witness for Jesus Christ will require a sacrifice on your part. Consider what the late Dr. Francis Schaeffer writes about sacrifice in his book *The Church at the End of the Twentieth Century:*

> If you think what God has done here at L'Abri [a chalet in Switzerland where Dr. Schaeffer ministered to those seeking to know about Christianity] is easy, you don't understand. It's a costly business. In about the first three years of L'Abri, all of our wedding presents were wiped out—our sheets were torn, holes were burned in our rugs, indeed once a whole curtain almost burned up from someone smoking in our living room. Everybody came to our table—it couldn't have happened any other way. Drugs came to our place, people vomited on our floors....[50]

Now, I'm not saying that this is going to happen to you and your home. But you will have to be willing to make some personal sacrifices as you reach out to others. Let's take a moment to consider the Samaritan again. What did he sacrifice to help the beaten traveler?

- *He sacrificed his possessions*—He bandaged the man's wounds, and poured oil and wine on the wounds.
- *He sacrificed his time*—He spent at least one day out of his life ministering to the man.
- *He sacrificed his finances*—He gave the innkeeper "two silver coins" (the equivalent of two days' wages) for the

> wounded man's immediate needs. He also gave the innkeeper a blank check and said, "Look after him, and when I return, I will reimburse you for any extra expense you may have" (verse 35).

How much are you willing to sacrifice to become a good neighbor? It may mean having lunch with an acquaintance and listening to him pour out his heart (a sacrifice of time). It may mean inviting a fellow worker to a ball game and paying for the tickets (a sacrifice of money). It may mean inviting your neighbors over to your house for a meal or dessert (a sacrifice of time and money). Whatever the sacrifice, it will be worthwhile! How much is a soul worth? It cost God the death of His only Son on the Cross. What's a few dollars or a little time in relation to eternity? Be willing to sacrifice of yourself—God did!

Principle #8: They are not the enemy—Some Christians have the mistaken idea that unbelievers are "the enemy." As a result, they avoid them, are afraid of them, and have little or nothing to do with them.

The Samaritan did not see the wounded Jew as his enemy. The robbers were the enemy, and the wounded man was the victim of the enemy. We rightly view victims of tragedy with great empathy and concern. So why don't we view the unbelievers around us in the same way? They are not the enemy. They are victims. They are slaves of Satan and sin (2 Timothy 2:26), and they can't help themselves (Romans 3:10-18).

Friend, we shouldn't fear unbelievers. We should pity them instead. Pray for them, and show them that you care for them. Take every opportunity to become their friend and neighbor.

Reaching Out to Others

"Who is my neighbor?" That's the question one man asked Jesus in Luke chapter 10. Jesus responded by telling the story of the Good Samaritan and the two religious leaders. When He finished, he then shot this question to the inquirer, "Which of these three do you think was a neighbor to the man who fell into the hands of robbers?"

The inquirer replied, "The one who had mercy on him."

Jesus then said, "Go and do likewise" (Luke 10:36-37).

Friend, that admonition applies to you and me as well. Become a neighbor—a *good* neighbor—by having mercy on the unbelievers around you...and reach out and touch someone....

Reach Out and Touch Someone

Reach out and touch a soul that is hungry;
Reach out and touch a spirit in despair;
Reach out and touch a life torn and dirty,
A man who is lonely if you care!

Reach out and touch that neighbor who hates you;
Reach out and touch that stranger who meets you;
Reach out and touch the brother who needs you;
Reach out and let the smile of God touch through you.

Reach out and touch a friend who is weary;
Reach out and touch a seeker unaware;
Reach out and touch, though touching means losing
A part of your own self if you dare!

Reach out and give your love to the loveless;
Reach out and make a home for the homeless;
Reach out and shed God's light in the darkness;
Reach out and let the smile of God touch through you.

—Charles F. Brown

It's been reported that George Mueller of Bristol, England, began to pray for the salvation of five personal friends. After five years, one of those friends came to Christ. After ten years, two more were saved. For 25 years he continued praying for the other two, and then the fourth was saved. Until his death, he did not cease to intercede for the conversion of the fifth. A few months after he died, the fifth man was saved. Mighty in its working is the righteous man's prayer.

17
A Heart That Builds Bridges

In your hearts set apart Christ as Lord.
Always be prepared to give an answer to everyone
who asks you to give the reason for the hope that you have.

—1 PETER 3:15

Men often tell me they don't know how to share their faith, or they don't think they know enough Bible or theology to be able to share their faith. For these reasons, they shy away from opportunities that might arise for reaching others for Christ.

It's true that skills and knowledge are important and that we should learn more of God's truth so we are better equipped to share our faith. But, my friend, it's not necessary for us to be a theologian before we can share about the most significant aspect of our life with those who are willing and eager to listen.

Sharing Your Testimony

The Example

I don't know how long you've been a Christian, but you've probably heard your pastor or other Christians talk about "sharing your testimony." Basically, your testimony is your story of how you became a Christian. And to show just how simple it is for us to share our testimony, I want to point you to another story, the account of the demon-possessed man in Mark 5:1-20. The short version of this man's demise is that he was tormented by a "legion" of demons. Jesus, in His mercy upon this poor man, cast the demons out of the man and sent them into a herd of pigs, which then ran down a hill into a lake and drowned.

The person I want to focus on in this event is the man. He was so thrilled to be free of the demons that he asked Jesus if he could follow Him. You might think Jesus would say, "Sure, come follow Me and learn some theology. Sit at My feet and let me tutor you for a few years until you are ready to share your testimony." Instead, Jesus told the man, "Go home to your family and tell them how much the Lord has done for you, and how he has had mercy on you" (Mark 5:19). Essentially, Jesus told the man to go home and share his testimony! Even as a new believer, this man had all he needed to testify of his experience with Jesus.

Now, let's observe the results of this man's obedience to Christ. The Bible tells us, "So the man went away and began to tell in the Decapolis [the man's home region] how much Jesus had done for him. And all the people were amazed" (verse 20).

What was the impact of his changed life? I believe we see it later on in Mark 7:31-8:9. Here, we read that Jesus was moving through a Gentile region outside of Israel. He had not been in this area before, nor was He well known here. But amazingly, Jesus arrives at this remote place to find a crowd of about 4,000 men (not to mention women and children) ready and waiting to hear His message!

Where did these people come from? I personally believe the man in Mark 5:1-20 had done exactly what Jesus had told him to do. I believe he had obediently told people "how much Jesus had done for him" (Mark 5:20). I believe he had simply shared his testimony. Therefore, those people showed up in a faraway place to see Jesus and to hear His message for themselves.

The Specifics

Brother, your personal testimony of Christ's work in your life is the greatest tool you have for reaching others for God. Why? Because it's about *your* life and *your* experience with Jesus Christ. It's personal. So no one can refute it. The fact that it happened to you makes it more meaningful to the people who know you.

Your personal testimony can be broken down into three parts:

- Part one—*What my life was like before I met Jesus Christ.*
- Part two—*How I met Jesus Christ.*
- Part three—*What my life has been like since meeting Jesus Christ.*

Now here's an assignment for you. Think back over your life and spend some time reflecting on the circumstances that led to your acceptance of Christ as your Savior. Then take note of the differences you and others have seen in your life since you came to Christ. Using the three-part breakdown for sharing your personal testimony, write out what happened to you.

Once you've done this, you are ready to carry out the apostle Peter's exhortation in 1 Peter 3:15: "Always be prepared to give an answer to everyone who asks you to give the reason for the hope that you have." Why not take a moment now to say a prayer of thanks to God? Also, ask Him to give you an opportunity to share the reason for your hope—*your personal testimony*—with someone this week.

Building Bridges

Some time ago I was told the story of a high-level official in a foreign government who enrolled his son in a college in America. Because it was a Christian college, there was a great excitement among the students as to who might have the opportunity to share the gospel with this young man and possibly see him come to Christ. Would it be the senior class president? The star athlete? The campus chaplain?

Well, the young man did come to Christ. But everyone was surprised to learn the identity of the person whom God used as His messenger. Tom was just an average guy, one you would never pick out of a crowd as someone with unusual skills or witnessing abilities. Later when someone asked Tom what happened, he said, "I simply built a bridge between my heart and his, and then Jesus walked across it."

Becoming a neighbor. Developing friendships. Building bridges. Friend, *this* is what it means to develop a heart for reaching others! You and I don't need to be pastors or Bible scholars in order to witness. But we do need to earn the right to be heard by those around us.

What are some ways that we can build bridges that will help transport the message of Jesus Christ from our heart to the hearts of others? Here are some suggestions to get you started or help you to continue building bridges. (We could even call this Bridge Building 101!)

Maintain your personal testimony—As you consistently endeavor to live your life for Jesus Christ, your workmates and neighbors will see His transforming work in you through...

- your passion for life
- your positive attitude
- your pursuit of purity

- your speech (which builds up rather than tears down)
- your excellent work ethic
- your faithful church involvement
- your marriage
- your children
- your home

Pray for unbelievers—Salvation is *God's* job. Witnessing is *our* job. And so is prayer. We build bridges...and at the same time, we pray for God to walk across those bridges into the hearts and lives of others. So...

1. Pray for specific individuals. Pray for your relatives, your workmates, and your neighbors.
2. Pray for open doors so you can share your testimony (Colossians 4:3).
3. Pray for wisdom about what you communicate (Colossians 4:5-6).
4. Pray for God to override your fears and give you boldness (Ephesians 6:19).

Observe the interests and hobbies of others—One of the best ways to build bridges is to participate in the interests of those you are befriending. I once heard of a man who took up rose gardening just so he could have a point of common interest with his neighbor, who was an avid rose gardener. To make a long story short, that neighbor is now an avid *Christian* rose gardener!

Relate the Bible to current issues—There's never been a better time in our history than now to discuss our uncertain times! Just pick up any newspaper—every day there are issues facing us that cry out for a biblical explanation. Look for opportunities to relate the Bible to current issues and show how relevant the Bible is to the latest world or national crisis.

Show genuine interest in others—Human nature is predominantly marked by selfishness. People care much more about themselves than they do about others. So show some genuine interest in others...remember birthdays, anniversaries, the names and concerns and interests of unbelievers, especially those at work. As you go out of your way to show that you care, they will begin to see you as a friend and come to see Christianity in a positive light.

Meet unbelievers in the middle—What do I mean by "in the middle"? You will meet very few non-Christians at your church. Sure, there will be visitors who wander in off the street or who are brought to church by a friend or neighbor. But for the most part, the unbelievers are out there—in your neighborhood...at the office...at the little league field. So meet them in the middle, on their turf. That doesn't mean it's OK to go to places that are illegal or immoral. It just means going to the places where your fellow citizens are. Get to know people where they live and play.

Invite unbelievers to participate in your hobbies and interests—Not only can you take an interest in the hobbies of unbelievers, but you can also invite them to join you. If you play golf, extend an invitation to someone to play golf with you. As that person observes your life "up close and personal" on the field of competition, hopefully he will see your life from a different perspective.

Involve yourself with unbelievers—One of the greatest ways to involve yourself with non-Christians is through your children's school or sports activities. Why not become a coach for your child's little league or soccer team? Can you think of a better way for unbelieving parents to see a Christian in action than as a coach of their child's team?

Another way to expose unbelievers to true Christianity is as a volunteer worker. The sky is the limit! Every service organization in your community needs help. Why not lend a helping hand? You will be a positive benefit to your community, as well as salt and light for the gospel.

Finally (and this one is much more demanding!), consider running for public office. Christian values need to be modeled in your community. While we should not take advantage of public office as a platform for promoting our faith, we can let our lives speak volumes by the manner in which we handle our civic duties. Become a leader in your community, and let your life affirm the Christian values that our country was founded on.

Giving an Answer for Your Hope

Not long after I accepted a position as Director of Placement at Talbot Seminary in Southern California, where I received my theology training, I was asked to attend a seminar on student life. One of the speakers had a Ph.D. in theology from an Eastern seminary. It wasn't long before I realized this person didn't have a clue about what it meant to have a personal relationship with Jesus Christ. So, during one of the lunch breaks, I sat with him and initiated a conversation about salvation and the gospel message. I will never forget this educated religious professor's response: "Well, what about the heathen in Africa?"

His question brings up one of the most common fears most people have about witnessing. They worry, "What if an unbeliever asks a theological question that I can't answer?" Well, the chances of that happening aren't too great, for there are only about seven basic questions that non-Christians generally ask as they grapple with the truth of the gospel. And would you believe it—my unbelieving-Ph.D.-in-theology friend asked the number-one question from that list!

You may be among those who are afraid of the questions that might come your way after you've built the bridges, developed the friendships, and become a good neighbor. Well, cheer up—that's a good thing. Hopefully, there *will* be questions! Witnessing is not a one-way street. Evangelism is not a monologue, but a dialogue. Evangelism is listening to other people; understanding their objections, fears, and questions; and then seeking to give solid biblical answers.

The Christian faith demands that we have enough compassion to learn the questions of our generation and go to the Bible for its answers. And to help you be prepared, I'm going to list the seven basic questions (objections) that unbelievers most often ask. Alongside each objection, I'll also provide the most basic scriptures that will help you with the answers. My prayer is that you have developed the kinds of friendships with others that will make them feel comfortable asking you one of these questions.

Seven Basic Objections to the Gospel

1. What about the heathen who have never heard the gospel? (Answer: Psalm 19:1; Romans 1:18-20)
2. Is Christ the only way to God? (Answer: John 14:6)
3. Why do the innocent suffer? (Answer: Romans 5:12)
4. How can miracles be possible? (Answer: John 1:1,14; John 3:2)
5. Isn't the Bible full of errors? (Answer: 2 Timothy 3:16; Hebrews 1:1-2; 2 Peter 1:20-21)
6. Isn't the Christian experience psychological? (Answer: Acts 9—the conversion of Paul; Romans 5:8-10)

7. Won't a good moral life get me to heaven? (Answer: Galatians 2:16; Titus 3:5; James 2:10)[51]

Showing That You Care

My friend, I pray that you will take on the task of building those bridges, making those friendships, and becoming a good neighbor so that you will have an opportunity to "give an answer to everyone who asks you to give the reason for the hope that you have" (1 Peter 3:15). The rewards are eternal, for those who come to Christ through your witness—both verbal and nonverbal—will become fellow citizens of heaven. Show people that you really care. Show them Christ's love through your love. Show them your heart!

Does Anyone Care?

A leading newspaper executive was visited by a local pastor. The man of God came right to the point as they shook hands. "My friend," he said, "I'm here to ask you to become a Christian."

The editor walked over to a window and for several minutes stood looking down into the street. The minister thought he had offended him. Finally the man turned, his face wet with tears. Taking his visitor's hand again, he said, "Thank you for your concern. Since I was a young boy at my mother's knee, not a single relative or business associate has ever taken an interest in my soul. I thought no one cared!"[52]

Part Three

The Purpose of God

18
God's Purpose in You

When David had served God's purpose in his own generation, he fell asleep.

—ACTS 13:36

This verse brings us full circle in the life of David. Do you remember how our study began, with God's epitaph that David was a man after His own heart (Acts 13:22)? When God sent the prophet Samuel to look for a new king, He cautioned him,

> The LORD does not look at the things man looks at. Man looks at the outward appearance, but the LORD looks at the *heart* (1 Samuel 16:7, emphasis added).

David began with few of the qualifications that are typically expected of a king—he was still a young boy caring for the family sheep. But David had a heart for God, and *that* was what God wanted.

As we have often noted, David experienced lapses in his walk with God. But unlike his predecessor, King Saul, there always came a point in time when David turned back to God with great remorse and sorrow. This repentant attitude was what made David usable to God. This sterling quality is what made David a man after God's own heart.

Following David's Footsteps

I'm so thankful that you have stayed with me throughout this book. My prayer is that you have come to understand that in everything, God looks on the heart. Your relationship with God has to do with your heart and your heart's desire. Like David, you probably have lapses. We all do! But you have a choice. You can choose to follow Saul, who didn't have a heart for God. When Saul lapsed into sin, he wasn't interested in doing what was right. He was only interested in pleasing himself. Saul wasn't concerned for God's will...only his own. But God was looking for obedience (1 Samuel 15:22), and God found that obedience in David.

Do you desire to have a heart of obedience as well? All through this book I've challenged you to develop a heart for God and for the things of God. Now, my friend, I have one final challenge: Whose example will you follow? Don't follow after Saul's example! Follow instead in David's footsteps. Give God your whole heart and your obedience. Then you, like David, will be a man God can—and will—use.

Pursuing God's Purpose

Back in chapter 1, I admitted that I was somewhat puzzled about God's epitaph for David because of David's lapses. But when we look at Acts 13:36, we can see the reason for God's words. This verse tells us,

> When David had served God's *purpose* in his own generation, he fell asleep (Acts 13:36, emphasis added).

God had a life purpose for David. David willingly followed God's purpose for his life and he fulfilled it. His heart for God allowed him to be used mightily by God to his own generation. He was used of God in spite of his shortcomings.

God has a life purpose for you. What an incredible opportunity you have available to you! You, like David, have a purpose. *Will you live out your purpose, or God's?* Wouldn't you want it to be said of you that you are serving the purpose of God? My guess is that you desire this as much as I do. What man of God wouldn't want to fulfill God's grand purpose for his life?

Well, dear brother, you can make God's purposes for you a reality in your life. How? Simply by living out God's priorities. You can't do anything about the past. But starting today, you can personally and positively affect this generation...*your* generation. And this positive effect will come naturally as you live out God's priorities for your life.

That's what we've been talking about in this book—living out God's purpose for you. The priorities we have discussed—related to our wives, our children, our church, our jobs, and our witness—serve as a great beginning to understanding God's purpose for our lives. I challenge you as I challenge myself: Seek God's help in fulfilling His purpose by reading your Bible, finding someone to disciple you, and desiring God's will with all your heart. Live out His priorities. And as you develop this seeking heart, you will have a marked effect on your family, your church, your workplace, and your neighborhood. Your generation will never be the same. And what's more, your striving toward fulfilling God's purpose will have a ripple effect on others for generations to come. May this living epitaph be true of your life:

(Your Name)

____

is a man after God's own heart
who is living out the purpose of God.

A Final Word

It gave me great joy to have some brothers come and tell about your faithfulness to the truth and how you continue to walk in the truth. I have no greater joy than to hear that my children are walking in the truth.

—3 JOHN 3-4

Well, it happened again. I had just come out of the post office and was sitting in the car while I opened the mail. And there it was—another letter...from a man...written to my wife! However, as in times past, I knew exactly what the letter would say. And sure enough, I was right. The letter was from a grateful husband and father. He was thanking my wife Elizabeth for writing her book *A Woman After God's Own Heart*. Evidently the biblical principles about a woman's priorities had transformed the man's wife, which in turned had transformed their marriage and their home.

As I sat there (in the rain of course...we live in the rainy Pacific Northwest), I could only thank God again for the transforming power of His Word. I could only praise Him as

I reminisced on my own journey of obedience to God's Word. I was grateful to the Lord once again for His amazing grace in my life and in my family's life.

And then I dared to dream. Could *A Man After God's Own Heart* have the same effect on men as Elizabeth's book had on women? Would I be able to communicate how obedience to God's Word has changed my life and can change other lives, too?

My prayer is that this book has encouraged you to become a man after God's own heart. My hope is that you have evaluated your relationship with God and have decided to make Him your first priority. This one decision alone will have a domino effect on all of your life!

It is also my prayer that, one day, I will receive a letter from a wife whose husband's life has been changed by *A Man After God's Own Heart*. It's my hope that she will send me a glowing testimonial of how these changes have had a positive impact on their marriage and family.

But more importantly, my hope is that *your* life is undergoing change right now—that...

- you have gone from being a nominal Christian to an avid follower of Jesus Christ,
- your love for your wife is stronger and more visible and vibrant than ever before,
- your devotion and attention to your children is impacting their lives,
- your commitment to your job has been revitalized,
- your love for the church has moved you to greater service, and

- your relatives and neighbors have made numerous comments on your transformed life, which, in turn, has transformed their lives.

Don't let me sit out in the rain reading my wife's mail from husbands who appreciate how their wives have changed. Start yourself on the path to becoming a man after God's own heart so *your* wife will want to give everyone (including me) a glowing report of God's transforming power in *your* life. I can't wait for that letter to arrive! What joy it will bring my heart to hear that you, a brother in Christ, desire to be faithful to the truth and to walk in the truth (3 John 3-4)!

STUDY GUIDE

Chapter 1—What Is Your Heart's Desire?

1. Why did God call David "a man after God's own heart"?

2. What does God look for in your life?

3. What does it mean to become a Christian?

4. What does 2 Corinthians 5:17 say about Christians?

5. What is your heart's desire for your life?

6. If you were to die today, what epitaph would you want on your grave marker?

Chapter 2—Desiring Spiritual Growth

1. What sets the Bible apart from all other books?

2. Why did God write the Bible?

3. What did Jesus promise in John 14:16-17, 26?

4. To become a strong, maturing man of God, what should be your first priority?

5. Look again at the section "The Impact of Growth" on pages 26-27. What one thing can you do this week to have a greater impact in each of these areas?

   Be a strong, maturing man of God—

Be a good husband—

Be a good father—

Be a caring coworker—

6. Read through John Wesley's prayer on page 28. What can you change or add to the prayer so it has more personal application to you?

Chapter 3—Making Spiritual Growth Happen

1. What do you enjoy most? Is it having a positive or negative effect on those closest to you? (Try your best to answer this not from your perspective, but through the eyes of others.)

2. Write out the three steps that would best help you in pursuing spiritual growth (see pages 33-38).

   Step 1—

   Step 2—

   Step 3—

3. Now jot down the strategies you will undertake with each one.

4. To grow spiritually strong, you need spiritual instruction from the Bible. Which of the growth methods on page 36 are you currently practicing? What new methods would you like to put into use?

5. What are the benefits of spiritual growth?

Chapter 4—The Marks of a Man After God's Own Heart, Part I

1. What is the bottom-line mark of God's man?

2. Name one area of your life in which you are struggling to be obedient. What immediate steps can you take to become more obedient in this area?

3. One key element of mastering the art of prayer is time. How important is prayer to you? Is that reflected in the time you spend in prayer? What are some ways you can develop a more consistent prayer life (consider the suggestions on page 49)?

4. What are some good places available to you for spending time in prayer?

5. What one truth from this chapter had the greatest impact on you, and why?

Chapter 5—The Marks of a Man After God's Own Heart, Part II

1. When you thank God for His blessings or express your love to Him, you are praising Him. What are some things you can thank (and praise) God for right now?

2. According to pages 55-57, what are six different ways we can praise God, or practice the presence of God?

3. Read Psalm 34:1. Is this true about you? Commit yourself to doing this for a full day. Then describe what effect this has on you and your day.

4. Who is our supreme example of what it means to be a servant?

5. Read Philippians 2:3-8. In what ways can you learn from the example of servanthood portrayed in these verses?

Chapter 6—A Heart That Loves Your Wife, Part I

1. According to pages 68-69, what are five specifics of Christ's love for the church?

2. Going through the five specifics one by one, how does your love for your wife compare to Christ's love for His church?

   Sacrificial love—

   Purifying love—

   Nurturing love—

   Enduring love—

Active love—

3. In what way can you show sacrifice to your wife today? What about every day?

4. What are some ways you've nurtured your wife in the past? What are two or three ways you can show nurture in the days ahead?

5. What are some simple yet meaningful ways you can show your wife that your love for her is an enduring love?

6. See the poem "Love" on page 74. Could your wife have written the words in this poem to describe your love for her? Why, or why not? And how can you change this?

Chapter 7—A Heart That Loves Your Wife, Part II

1. On page 78 is an encouragement for you to write a list of the things you did to nurture your relationship with the woman who became your wife (if you're not yet married, then write a list of what you *could* do). How many of these things are you presently doing? Commit to doing more of them again.

2. How much time did you spend with your wife this last week? In what ways can you make it very clear that she is truly a priority to you?

3. Do you truly focus on your wife when you're alone with her? What are some ways you can make sure you are giving her your full attention?

4. On pages 82-83 is a list of ways to become a better listener. How many of these do you carry out regularly? Can you add more items to the list?

5. Telling your wife you love her is a vital part of keeping your marriage healthy. When was the last time you affirmed your wedding vows to her?

6. What one thing can you do this week to let your wife know you're still committed to your vows?

Chapter 8—A Heart That Leads Your Wife

1. If you are a husband and father, what does God hold you responsible for?

2. What is the most significant way you can encourage your wife's spiritual growth?

3. What are some additional ways you can nurture your wife's spiritual growth and be a "spiritual cheerleader"?

4. Do you pray daily for your wife's protection and purity? List some specific ways you can do this.

5. Do you provide spiritual leadership by taking time to pray together with your wife? When is a good time for you to pray as a couple, and what are some things you could pray about together?

6. By your actions or lack of actions, you may be telling your wife, "I don't love you." What two or three changes can you make to ensure that doesn't happen? Commit yourself to carrying out those changes.

Chapter 9—A Heart That Loves Your Children

1. What is one key to your success as a father (see page 102)?

2. As your heart goes, so goes your family. Take some time now to examine your heart, and lift up your concerns and requests to God.

3. According to page 104, what is the fundamental task of parenting? In what ways can a father carry out this task?

4. Read again the section "Passing On a Love for God" (see pages 104-06). What made the greatest impression on you as you revisited these words?

5. List five ways you can influence your children (see page 107). What are some additional ways you can influence them?

Chapter 10—A Heart That Leads Your Children

1. Who ultimately is responsible for your children's hearts?

2. What gets in the way of your care for your children? How can you rearrange your priorities?

3. On a scale of 1 to 10, how would you rate your consistency as a godly example in front of your children? What is one area in which you would like to improve?

4. Are you struggling with your role as the spiritual leader of your family? Ask God to help you find a role model who can help you.

5. What are the essentials of providing good discipline to your children?

6. Are you taking advantage of the privilege of praying for your children? List some things you can start praying for right now. Make a habit of praying for your children daily!

Chapter 11—A Heart That Is Diligent at Work

1. What misconception do many people have about work?

2. According to the passages on pages 126-27, what are some things the Bible teaches us about work?

3. In what ways is work beneficial?

4. How does the fact that work is a calling affect your attitude about your job (see pages 128-29)?

5. How are you doing as an ambassador for Christ in your workplace?

6. What are some specific ways you can bring glory to God as you carry out your job tasks?

Chapter 12—A Heart That Glorifies God at Work, Part I

1. Based on the example of King David, what do we need to avoid doing at work so that we don't dishonor God?

2. What are some ways you can exercise greater diligence on the job?

3. The Bible calls all Christians to have a servant's heart. List here the six ways of becoming a better servant at work (see page 140).

4. What are some ways you can learn to do your job better? Is there a specific step you can begin taking right now?

5. Would you describe yourself as satisfied with your progress at work, or as someone who stretches toward greater growth? Ask God to help you determine ways you can stretch more.

Chapter 13—A Heart That Glorifies God at Work, Part II

1. Go through the list of virtues exhibited by Boaz in his life and work habits. Which of these virtues stood out to you? Which of them can you begin to implement in your life?

2. What kind of discontentment is good, and what kind is not good?

3. When the apostle Paul was in prison, what was his contentment *not* based on? What *was* it based on? What would this kind of contentment look like in your life?

4. According to page 152, what do you need to remember in order to know contentment at work?

5. What are some ways you can be a model of excellence at work?

6. How would your boss rate you in the following areas?

   Integrity—

   Faithfulness—

   Punctuality—

   Workmanship—

   Attitude—

   Enthusiasm—

7. Spend time in prayer now, and ask God to help your every action at work bring glory to Him.

Chapter 14—A Heart That Loves the Church

1. What are some things Christ taught about the church in the book of Ephesians?

2. What are the privileges of your membership in the church, Christ's body?

3. Consider the responsibilities of church membership as listed on page 160. What are two or three areas in which you would like to experience greater growth?

4. As a member of your church, how can you improve on your usefulness in the following areas?

   Faithful attendance—

   Giving—

Prayer—

Service—

5. If you are actively serving in your church, ask God to help you carry out your responsibilities with diligence. If you are not serving, ask Him to lead you to an area of service.

Chapter 15—A Heart That Serves the Church

1. Review the list of simple things you can do that would mean a lot to others in your church (see page 167). What two or three things can you do this week or month? Write them down, and resolve to carry them out.

2. What are the basic principles Scripture teaches regarding spiritual gifts?

3. Why does God give spiritual gifts?

4. What are the steps to finding out your area of spiritual giftedness?

5. According to page 174, what are some ways you can begin making use of your giftedness?

6. Read through 1 Timothy 3:1-7 and Titus 1:6-9 and the leadership qualities listed in those passages. Are you ready to "kick it up a notch"? What qualities need your immediate attention?

Chapter 16—A Heart That Reaches Out

1. To date, how would you rate your job performance—and your attitude toward your job—on a scale of one to ten, with ten being the highest possible score?

2. What are some ways you can "earn the right" to talk to your co-workers about Christ and the meaning of life?

3. The example of the Good Samaritan teaches us that love takes the initiative. Who is one person you can reach out to this week, and how can you show Christlike love for that person?

4. Is there an unlovely person who has made life difficult for you? Make a commitment to pray daily for this person for 30 days, and ask God to help you see this person through His eyes.

5. What is our tendency when we encounter someone who is struggling with deep hurt or pain? How should we respond?

6. What did the Good Samaritan sacrifice when he helped the beaten traveler?

7. Think of two or three workmates who need to know Jesus Christ. Write their names here. Then make a deliberate effort to become a better neighbor by "developing a heart that reaches out."

Chapter 17—A Heart That Builds Bridges

1. Why are we sometimes shy about sharing our faith?

2. What does it mean to "share your testimony"?

3. What are the three parts of a testimony?

4. Using the three-part outline below, briefly write your testimony. Then ask God to bring to you someone whom you can share it with.

   What my life was like before I met Jesus Christ—

   How I met Jesus Christ—

What my life has been like since meeting Jesus Christ—

5. According to pages 196-98, what are eight ways we can build bridges?

6. If you are not able to answer questions an unbeliever might ask about the Christian faith, what are some good ways you can help him or her find answers?

Chapter 18—God's Purpose in You

1. In regard to lapses in one's walk with God, what did King David do that set him apart from King Saul and made him useful to God?

2. How do you respond to the fact God has a purpose for your life?

3. Consider all that you do during an average day. Which are you doing more: living out your purposes, or God's?

4. How can you make God's purposes for you a reality in your life?

5. Take time to pray now and commit yourself to growing more and more in God's purposes in your life!

How to Study the Bible—Some Practical Tips

One of the noblest pursuits a child of God can embark upon is to get to know and understand God better. The best way we can accomplish this is to look carefully at the book He has written, the Bible, which communicates who He is and His plan for mankind. There are a number of ways we can study the Bible, but one of the most effective and simple approaches to reading and understanding God's Word involves three simple steps:

Step 1: Observation—*What does the passage say?*

Step 2: Interpretation—*What does the passage mean?*

Step 3: Application—*What am I going to do about what the passage says and means?*

Observation is the first and most important step in the process. As you read the Bible text, you need to *look* carefully at what is said, and how it is said. Look for:

- *Terms, not words.* Words can have many meanings, but terms are words used in a specific way in a specific context. (For instance, the word *trunk* could apply to a tree, a car, or a storage box. However, when you read, "That tree has a very large trunk," you know exactly what the word means, which makes it a term.)

- *Structure.* If you look at your Bible, you will see that the text has units called *paragraphs* (indented or marked ¶). A paragraph is a complete unit of thought. You can discover the content of the author's message by noting and understanding each paragraph unit.
- *Emphasis.* The amount of space or the number of chapters or verses devoted to a specific topic will reveal the importance of that topic (for example, note the emphasis of Romans 9–11 and Psalm 119).
- *Repetition.* This is another way an author demonstrates that something is important. One reading of 1 Corinthians 13, where the author uses the word "love" nine times in only 13 verses, communicates to us that love is the focal point of these 13 verses.
- *Relationships between ideas.* Pay close attention to certain relationships that appear in the text, for example:

  —Cause-and-effect: "Well done, good and faithful servant; you were faithful over a few things, I will make you ruler over many things" (Matthew 25:21).

  —Ifs and thens: "If My people who are called by My name will humble themselves, and pray and seek My face, and turn from their wicked ways, then I will hear from heaven and forgive their sin and heal their land" (2 Chronicles 7:14).

  —Questions and answers: "Who is the King of glory? The Lord strong and mighty" (Psalm 24:8).

- *Comparisons and contrasts.* For example, "You have heard that it was said...but I say to you..." (Matthew 5:21).
- *Literary form.* The Bible is literature, and the three main types of literature in the Bible are discourse (the epistles), prose (Old Testament history), and poetry (the Psalms). Considering the type of literature makes a great deal of difference when you read and interpret the Scriptures.
- *Atmosphere.* The author had a particular reason or burden for writing each passage, chapter, and book. Be sure you notice the mood or tone or urgency of the writing.

After you have considered these things, you then are ready to ask the "Wh" questions:

Who? Who are the people in this passage?

What? What is happening in this passage?

Where? Where is this story taking place?

When? What time (of day, of the year, in history) is it?

Asking these four "Wh" questions can help you notice terms and identify atmosphere. The answers will also enable you to use your imagination to recreate the scene you're reading about.

As you answer the "Wh" questions and imagine the event, you'll probably come up with some questions of your own. Asking those additional questions for understanding will help to build a bridge between observation (the first step) and interpretation (the second step) of the Bible study process.

Interpretation is discovering the meaning of a passage, the author's main thought or idea. Answering the questions that arise during observation will help you in the process of interpretation. Five clues (called "the five C's") can help you determine the author's main point(s):

- *Context.* You can answer 75 percent of your questions about a passage when you read the text. Reading the text involves looking at the near context (the verse immediately before and after) as well as the far context (the paragraph or the chapter that precedes and/or follows the passage you're studying).

- *Cross-references.* Let Scripture interpret Scripture. That is, let other passages in the Bible shed light on the passage you are looking at. At the same time, be careful not to assume that the same word or phrase in two different passages means the same thing.

- *Culture.* The Bible was written long ago, so when we interpret it, we need to understand it from the writers' cultural context.

- *Conclusion.* Having answered your questions for understanding by means of context, cross-reference, and culture, you can make a preliminary statement of the passage's meaning. Remember that if your passage consists of more than one paragraph, the author may be presenting more than one thought or idea.

- *Consultation.* Reading books known as commentaries, which are written by Bible scholars, can help you interpret Scripture.

Application is why we study the Bible. We want our lives to change; we want to be obedient to God and to grow more like Jesus Christ. After we have observed a passage and interpreted or understood it to the best of our ability, we must then apply its truth to our own life.

You'll want to ask the following questions of every passage of Scripture you study:

- How does the truth revealed here affect my relationship with God?

- How does this truth affect my relationship with others?
- How does this truth affect me?
- How does this truth affect my response to the enemy, Satan?

The application step is not completed by simply answering these questions; the key is *putting into practice* what God has taught you in your study. Although at any given moment you cannot be consciously applying *every*thing you're learning in Bible study, you can be consciously applying *some*thing. And when you work on applying a truth to your life, God will bless your efforts by, as noted earlier, conforming you to the image of Jesus Christ.

Helpful Bible Study Resources:

Concordance—Young's or Strong's

Bible dictionary—Unger's or Holman's

Webster's dictionary

The Zondervan Pictorial Encyclopedia of the Bible

Manners and Customs of the Bible, James M. Freeman

Books on Bible Study:

The Joy of Discovery, Oletta Wald

Enjoy Your Bible, Irving L. Jensen

How to Read the Bible for All Its Worth, Gordon Fee & Douglas Stuart

A Layman's Guide to Interpreting the Bible, W. Henrichsen

Living by the Book, Howard G. Hendricks

A One-Year Daily Bible Reading Plan

January	Genesis
❑ 1	1–3
❑ 2	4–7
❑ 3	8–11
❑ 4	12–15
❑ 5	16–18
❑ 6	19–22
❑ 7	23–27
❑ 8	28–30
❑ 9	31–34
❑ 10	35–38
❑ 11	39–41
❑ 12	42–44
❑ 13	45–47
❑ 14	48–50
	Exodus
❑ 15	1–4
❑ 16	5–7
❑ 17	8–11
❑ 18	12–14
❑ 19	15–18
❑ 20	19–21
❑ 21	22–24
❑ 22	25–28
❑ 23	29–31
❑ 24	32–34

❑ 25	35–37
❑ 26	38–40
	Leviticus
❑ 27	1–3
❑ 28	4–6
❑ 29	7–9
❑ 30	10–13
❑ 31	14–16
February	
❑ 1	17–20
❑ 2	21–23
❑ 3	24–27
	Numbers
❑ 4	1–2
❑ 5	3–4
❑ 6	5–6
❑ 7	7–8
❑ 8	9–10
❑ 9	11–13
❑ 10	14–15
❑ 11	16–17
❑ 12	18–19
❑ 13	20–21
❑ 14	22–23
❑ 15	24–26
❑ 16	27–29
❑ 17	30–32
❑ 18	33–36
	Deuteronomy
❑ 19	1–2
❑ 20	3–4
❑ 21	5–7
❑ 22	8–10
❑ 23	11–13
❑ 24	14–16
❑ 25	17–20

❑ 26	21–23
❑ 27	24–26
❑ 28	27–28

March

❑ 1	29–30
❑ 2	31–32
❑ 3	33–34
	Joshua
❑ 4	1–4
❑ 5	5–7
❑ 6	8–10
❑ 7	11–14
❑ 8	15–17
❑ 9	18–21
❑ 10	22–24
	Judges
❑ 11	1–3
❑ 12	4–6
❑ 13	7–9
❑ 14	10–12
❑ 15	13–15
❑ 16	16–18
❑ 17	19–21
	Ruth
❑ 18	1–4
	1 Samuel
❑ 19	1–3
❑ 20	4–6
❑ 21	7–9
❑ 22	10–12
❑ 23	13–14
❑ 24	15–16
❑ 25	17–18
❑ 26	19–20
❑ 27	21–23

❑ 28	24–26
❑ 29	27–29
❑ 30	30–31
	2 Samuel
❑ 31	1–3

April

❑ 1	4–6
❑ 2	7–10
❑ 3	11–13
❑ 4	14–15
❑ 5	16–17
❑ 6	18–20
❑ 7	21–22
❑ 8	23–24
	1 Kings
❑ 9	1–2
❑ 10	3–5
❑ 11	6–7
❑ 12	8–9
❑ 13	10–12
❑ 14	13–15
❑ 15	16–18
❑ 16	19–20
❑ 17	21–22
	2 Kings
❑ 18	1–3
❑ 19	4–6
❑ 20	7–8
❑ 21	9–11
❑ 22	12–14
❑ 23	15–17
❑ 24	18–19
❑ 25	20–22
❑ 26	23–25

1 Chronicles

❑ 27 1–2
❑ 28 3–5
❑ 29 6–7
❑ 30 8–10

May

❑ 1 11–13
❑ 2 14–16
❑ 3 17–19
❑ 4 20–22
❑ 5 23–25
❑ 6 26–27
❑ 7 28–29

2 Chronicles

❑ 8 1–4
❑ 9 5–7
❑ 10 8–10
❑ 11 11–14
❑ 12 15–18
❑ 13 19–21
❑ 14 22–25
❑ 15 26–28
❑ 16 29–31
❑ 17 32–33
❑ 18 34–36

Ezra

❑ 19 1–4
❑ 20 5–7
❑ 21 8–10

Nehemiah

❑ 22 1–3
❑ 23 4–7
❑ 24 8–10
❑ 25 11–13

	Esther
❑ 26	1–3
❑ 27	4–7
❑ 28	8–10
	Job
❑ 29	1–4
❑ 30	5–8
❑ 31	9–12
June	
❑ 1	13–16
❑ 2	17–20
❑ 3	21–24
❑ 4	25–30
❑ 5	31–34
❑ 6	35–38
❑ 7	39–42
	Psalms
❑ 8	1–8
❑ 9	9–17
❑ 10	18–21
❑ 11	22–28
❑ 12	29–34
❑ 13	35–39
❑ 14	40–44
❑ 15	45–50
❑ 16	51–56
❑ 17	57–63
❑ 18	64–69
❑ 19	70–74
❑ 20	75–78
❑ 21	79–85
❑ 22	86–90
❑ 23	91–98
❑ 24	99–104
❑ 25	105–107
❑ 26	108–113

- ❑ 27 114–118
- ❑ 28 119
- ❑ 29 120–134
- ❑ 30 135–142

July

- ❑ 1 143–150

Proverbs

- ❑ 2 1–3
- ❑ 3 4–7
- ❑ 4 8–11
- ❑ 5 12–15
- ❑ 6 16–18
- ❑ 7 19–21
- ❑ 8 22–24
- ❑ 9 25–28
- ❑ 10 29–31

Ecclesiastes

- ❑ 11 1–4
- ❑ 12 5–8
- ❑ 13 9–12

Song of Solomon

- ❑ 14 1–4
- ❑ 15 5–8

Isaiah

- ❑ 16 1–4
- ❑ 17 5–8
- ❑ 18 9–12
- ❑ 19 13–15
- ❑ 20 16–20
- ❑ 21 21–24
- ❑ 22 25–28
- ❑ 23 29–32
- ❑ 24 33–36
- ❑ 25 37–40
- ❑ 26 41–43

❑ 27	44–46
❑ 28	47–49
❑ 29	50–52
❑ 30	53–56
❑ 31	57–60

August

❑ 1	61–63
❑ 2	64–66
	Jeremiah
❑ 3	1–3
❑ 4	4–6
❑ 5	7–9
❑ 6	10–12
❑ 7	13–15
❑ 8	16–19
❑ 9	20–22
❑ 10	23–25
❑ 11	26–29
❑ 12	30–31
❑ 13	32–34
❑ 14	35–37
❑ 15	38–40
❑ 16	41–44
❑ 17	45–48
❑ 18	49–50
❑ 19	51–52
	Lamentations
❑ 20	1–2
❑ 21	3–5
	Ezekiel
❑ 22	1–4
❑ 23	5–8
❑ 24	9–12
❑ 25	13–15
❑ 26	16–17
❑ 27	18–20

❑ 28	21–23
❑ 29	24–26
❑ 30	27–29
❑ 31	30–31

September

❑ 1	32–33
❑ 2	34–36
❑ 3	37–39
❑ 4	40–42
❑ 5	43–45
❑ 6	46–48
	Daniel
❑ 7	1–2
❑ 8	3–4
❑ 9	5–6
❑ 10	7–9
❑ 11	10–12
	Hosea
❑ 12	1–4
❑ 13	5–9
❑ 14	10–14
❑ 15	**Joel**
	Amos
❑ 16	1–4
❑ 17	5–9
❑ 18	**Obadiah and Jonah**
	Micah
❑ 19	1–4
❑ 20	5–7
❑ 21	**Nahum**
❑ 22	**Habakkuk**
❑ 23	**Zephaniah**
❑ 24	**Haggai**

	Zechariah
❑ 25	1–4
❑ 26	5–9
❑ 27	10–14
❑ 28	**Malachi**
	Matthew
❑ 29	1–4
❑ 30	5–7

October

❑ 1	8–9
❑ 2	10–11
❑ 3	12–13
❑ 4	14–16
❑ 5	17–18
❑ 6	19–20
❑ 7	21–22
❑ 8	23–24
❑ 9	25–26
❑ 10	27–28
	Mark
❑ 11	1–3
❑ 12	4–5
❑ 13	6–7
❑ 14	8–9
❑ 15	10–11
❑ 16	12–13
❑ 17	14
❑ 18	15–16
	Luke
❑ 19	1–2
❑ 20	3–4
❑ 21	5–6
❑ 22	7–8
❑ 23	9–10
❑ 24	11–12
❑ 25	13–14

❑ 26	15–16
❑ 27	17–18
❑ 28	19–20
❑ 29	21–22
❑ 30	23–24
	John
❑ 31	1–3

November

❑ 1	4–5
❑ 2	6–7
❑ 3	8–9
❑ 4	10–11
❑ 5	12–13
❑ 6	14–16
❑ 7	17–19
❑ 8	20–21
	Acts
❑ 9	1–3
❑ 10	4–5
❑ 11	6–7
❑ 12	8–9
❑ 13	10–11
❑ 14	12–13
❑ 15	14–15
❑ 16	16–17
❑ 17	18–19
❑ 18	20–21
❑ 19	22–23
❑ 20	24–26
❑ 21	27–28
	Romans
❑ 22	1–3
❑ 23	4–6
❑ 24	7–9
❑ 25	10–12
❑ 26	13–14
❑ 27	15–16

	1 Corinthians
❑ 28	1–4
❑ 29	5–7
❑ 30	8–10
December	
❑ 1	11–13
❑ 2	14–16
	2 Corinthians
❑ 3	1–4
❑ 4	5–9
❑ 5	10–13
	Galatians
❑ 6	1–3
❑ 7	4–6
	Ephesians
❑ 8	1–3
❑ 9	4–6
❑ 10	**Philippians**
❑ 11	**Colossians**
❑ 12	**1 Thessalonians**
❑ 13	**2 Thessalonians**
❑ 14	**1 Timothy**
❑ 15	**2 Timothy**
❑ 16	**Titus and Philemon**
	Hebrews
❑ 17	1–4
❑ 18	5–8
❑ 19	9–10
❑ 20	11–13
❑ 21	**James**
❑ 22	**1 Peter**
❑ 23	**2 Peter**
❑ 24	**1 John**
❑ 25	**2, 3 John, Jude**

	Revelation
❑ 26	1–3
❑ 27	4–8
❑ 28	9–12
❑ 29	13–16
❑ 30	17–19
❑ 31	20–22

Notes

1. J. Oswald Sanders, *Spiritual Leadership* (Chicago: Moody Press, 1980), p. 18.
2. Eleanor L. Doan, *The Speaker's Sourcebook* (Grand Rapids: Zondervan Publishing House, 1977), p. 96.
3. Kenneth W. Osbeck, *Amazing Grace* (Grand Rapids: Kregel Publications, 1990), p. 170.
4. D. L. Moody, *Notes from My Bible* (Grand Rapids: Baker Book House, 1979), p. 199.
5. Robert Van de Weyer, ed., *The Harper Collins Book of Prayers* (Edison, NJ: Castle Books, 1997), p. 388.
6. By George Liddell, cited in Sanders, *Spiritual Leadership*, pp. 17-18.
7. J. C. Ryle, in Terry W. Glaspey, *Pathway to the Heart of God* (Eugene, OR: Harvest House Publishers, 1998), p. 151.
8. Sanders, *Spiritual Leadership*, p. 123.
9. Glaspey, *Pathway to the Heart of God*, p. 151.
10. John Oxenham as cited in J. Allan Petersen, *For Men Only* (Wheaton, IL: Tyndale House Publishers, 1974), p. i.
11. Source unknown.
12. Herbert Lockyer, *All the Promises of the Bible* (Grand Rapids: Zondervan Publishing House, 1962), p. 10.
13. Richard Mayhue, *Seeking God* (Fearn, Great Britain: Christian Focus Publications, 2000), p. 148.
14. Stuart Scott, *The Exemplary Husband* (Bemidji, MN: Focus Publishing, Inc., 2000), p. 116.
15. Ibid.
16. Cited from *The Best Loved Poems of the American People,* Hazel Fellman, ed. (New York: Garden City Books, 1936).

17. Kenneth Kilinski, as cited by Roy B. Zuck, *The Speaker's Quote Book* (Grand Rapids: Kregel Publications, 1997), p. 240.
18. Dwight Small, as cited by Sherwood Eliot Wirt and Kersten Beckstrom, *Topical Encyclopedia of Living Quotations* (Minneapolis: Bethany House Publishers, 1982), p. 81.
19. Author unknown, as cited by J. Allen Petersen, ed., *For Men Only,* p. 69.
20. John MacArthur, *The MacArthur Study Bible* (Nashville, TN: Word Publishing, 1997), p. 1944.
21. Christopher N. Bacorn, "Dear Dads: Save Your Sons," *Newsweek* (December 7, 1992), p. 13.
22. Tedd Tripp, *Shepherding a Child's Heart* (Wapwallopen, PA: Shepherd Press, 1995), p. 20.
23. Dennis and Dawn Wilson, *Christian Parenting in the Information Age* (TriCord Publishing, P.O. Box 951, West Jordan, Utah), p. 192.
24. Tripp, *Shepherding a Child's Heart*, p. 22.
25. Richard Baxter, as cited by Wilson, *Christian Parenting in the Information Age*, p. 186.
26. J. Daniel Banon, as cited by Zuck, *The Speaker's Quote Book*, p. 51.
27. J. I. Packer, *A Quest for Godliness* (Wheaton, IL: Crossway Books, 1990), p. 270.
28. Tripp, *Shepherding a Child's Heart*, p. 23.
29. John MacArthur, *Successful Christian Parenting* (Nashville, TN: Word Publishing, 1998), pp. 134-135.
30. Benjamin R. De Jong, *Uncle Ben's Quotebook* (Grand Rapids: Baker Book House, 1977), p. 275.
31. John Trent, as cited in William Nix, *Transforming Your Workplace for Christ* (Nashville, TN: Broadman & Holman Publishers, 1997), p. xii.
32. Petersen, ed., *For Men Only*, p. 125.
33. Ibid.
34. John MacArthur, *Rediscovering Pastoral Ministry* (Nashville, TN: Word Publishing, 1995).
35. Nix, *Transforming Your Workplace for Christ,* p. 2.
36. Unknown author, as cited by Petersen, *For Men Only*, p. 132.
37. Petersen, *For Men Only*, p. 24.
38. Kent Hughes, *Disciplines of a Godly Man*, (Wheaton, IL: Crossway Books, 1991), p. 140. Emphasis added.
39. Jeremiah Burroughs, *The Rare Jewel of Christian Contentment* (Carlisle, PA: Banner of Truth Trust, 2000), p. 42.

40. Gary Inrig, *A Call to Excellence* (Wheaton, IL: Victor Books, 1985), p. 87.
41. Don Baker, *Pain's Hidden Purpose* (Portland, OR: Multnomah Press, 1984), pp. 86-89.
42. Charles R. Swindoll, *Growing Strong Through the Seasons of Life* (Grand Rapids, MI: Zondervan Publishing House, 1983), p. 66-67.
43. Hughes, *Disciplines of a Godly Man,* p. 140. Emphases added.
44. "I Love Thy Kingdom, Lord!" hymn by Timothy Dwight.
45. Doan, *The Speaker's Sourcebook,* p. 223.
46. G. Abbott-Smith, *A Manual Greek Lexicon of the New Testament* (Edinburgh: T&T Clark, 1973), p. 346.
47. Ibid., p. 68.
48. "Rise Up, O Men of God!" hymn by William Merrill.
49. Arthur McPhee, *Friendship Evangelism* (Grand Rapids: Zondervan Publishing House, 1979).
50. Francis Schaeffer, *The Church at the End of the Twentieth Century,* (Downers Grove, IL: InterVarsity Press, 1970).
51. Adapted from Paul Little, *How to Give Away Your Faith* (Downers Grove, IL: InterVarsity Press, 1973), pp. 67-80.
52. From an unknown issue of *The Daily Bread.*

Personal Notes

Personal Notes

An Invitation to Write

If you would like to receive more information about other ministry resources produced by Jim George, or if you want to share how *A Man After God's Own Heart* has impacted your life, you can write to him at:

Jim George
P.O. Box 2879
Belfair, WA 98528

Toll-free fax/phone: 1-800-542-4611
www.JimGeorge.com